Chocolate

Chocolate

Children's Books by Frances Park and Ginger Park

My Freedom Trip: A Child's Escape from North Korea
The Royal Bee
Where on Earth Is My Bagel?
Good-bye, 382 Shin Dang Dong
The Have a Good Day Cafe

Novel by Frances Park and Ginger Park

To Swim Across the World

Novels by Frances Park

Hotline Heaven
When My Sister Was Cleopatra Moon

Chocolate

Frances Park and Ginger Park

Chocolate

A True Story of Two Sisters,
Tons of Treats, and the
Little Shop That Could

Thomas Dunne Books
St. Martin's Press  New York

The names and identifying characteristics of some individuals depicted in this book have been changed.

CHOCOLATE CHOCOLATE. Copyright © 2011 by Frances Park and Ginger Park. All rights reserved. Printed in the United States of America. For information, address St. Martin's Press, 175 Fifth Avenue, New York, N.Y. 10010.

www.thomasdunnebooks.com

www.stmartins.com

Design by Kathryn Parise

LIBRARY OF CONGRESS CATALOGING-IN-PUBLICATION DATA

Park, Frances, 1955–
    Chocolate Chocolate : the true story of two sisters, tons of
treats, and the little shop that could / Frances Park and Ginger
Park. — 1st ed.
        p. cm.
    ISBN 978-0-312-65293-7
    1. Chocolate Chocolate (Firm)   2. Park, Frances, 1955–   3. Park,
Ginger.   4. Chocolate industry—United States—History.   5. Candy
industry—United States—History.   6. Chocolate candy—United
States—History.   I. Park, Ginger.   II. Title.
    HD9200.U54C467 2011
    381'.456639209753—dc22

                                                        2011002714

First Edition: May 2011

10   9   8   7   6   5   4   3   2   1

To the Milk Boy

Contents

x

Contents

Chocolate

~~~~~~~~~~

Chocolate

Prologue

October 28, 2008. It seemed like business as usual at Chocolate Chocolate, but that night, after a quarter century, the lights would go out and stay out in our little shop, a shop we'd breathed all our dreams into nearly all our adult lives. Here we had embraced friendships, romance, children, and twenty-five years of customers who came through our doors as strangers and left as friends. But without the chocolate dream, there would be no story.

For us, chocolate proved an elixir that could soften all the blows of life: coping with our father's untimely death, losing our small inheritance to a contractor who left our shop in shambles, praying for love when there was none.

And now this.

No time for tears, it was a whirlwind day of chatting-laughing-gossiping with our regulars, many of whom had tripped in to bid us a fond farewell.

Amanda—also known as "Lips" for her perfect pout—began picking out her small bag o' goodies. "I still can't believe you're closing."

"A day for bittersweet chocolate," Francie consoled her.

"What kind of world do we live in," Lips cried, "when a chocolate shop loses its lease?"

"Look, it's not the end of the world," Ginger said, hope in her voice.

Or was it?

Boxing customers' bonbons while sneaking our own distracted us from the weight of the day. After all these years, chocolate, like a magic kiss, still had that effect. As dusk fell, we shared a moment with Lee, a big-hearted attorney.

"I couldn't miss your last day," he said, smiling. "My wife would never forgive me."

Lee's wife loved our dark glossy squares of chocolate, each one wrapped like a little gift from her husband. And even though he could find these delicious morsels elsewhere, we always sensed that Lee would follow us to the ends of the earth for our squares. Maybe that was just wishful thinking. We took a picture of him, just in case.

"Thanks, ladies—and good luck," he said, out the door.

"Good-bye." We waved.

At closing hour, nostalgia crept up on us. Would we be able to breathe life into a new home for our sweetshop and carry on the dream? We were older now, not the two young women who blindly went into business so long ago, la-di-da-ing into work on that first Valentine's Day in 1984, no idea that hundreds of men were already lined up at our doors and around the block. Had we become, like our shop, a little worn? Did we still really have the drive, the want-to, the *haul,* to start over? Only time would tell.

Francie took a deep breath.

"Lights out, Ginge."

Chapter 1

Baci Kiss

*Starry foil wraps velvety dark chocolate
around a creamy hazelnut nugget
and a love note to remember*

January 11, 1984.

"Lights on, Ginge."

On a bitterly cold day in the nation's capital—a day so cold the statues were cracking—our moods matched the sky. Gray. In a makeshift shop held together with temporary glass panes so thin we could feel the wind, our lights went on for the first time.

Our opening day felt anything but grand.

Ginger shivered in her blue wool coat. She had worn her brand-new silk dress for nothing; no coats were coming off today. Francie's hair, poofed to perfection, was frozen in place, and her chandelier earrings hung like icicles. The seven years that separated us were obvious even in the way Ginger scooted closer to her big sister in faux fur, hoping to share a little body heat. It felt like our general contractor had neglected to put in a heating system. And where was our sign?

Did the fool do *anything* right?

We burst into a duet of four-letter words, climaxing with murderous cries:

"I hate him!"

"I hope he goes to hell!"

Let's face it: There are times when only chocolate can make a bad day better. That's when you summon the most luminous piece of chocolate in the shop, one that sings to you. That *chocolat du jour*. After mulling, Francie claimed a royal blue box from the shelves, loosening the white chiffon ribbon and peeling off the seal. The lid lifted up like a cigar box, revealing rows of bonbons dressed up in silver foil with blue stars. Nugget shaped, these were the world-class Perugina confections known as Baci ("kiss" in Italian). Pure opera.

"Dig in, Ginge."

One Baci for Ginger—*pluck*. One Baci for Francie—*pluck*.

Even unwrapping our Bacis was an exquisite affair. The love notes tucked inside the foil were almost as comforting as the creamy-crunchy hazelnut chocolate itself—we were both promised exciting romance in the near future. Since neither of us had much of a love life going on, the Baci tasted twice as nice. Life just got a *little* grander.

The Reagan era in Washington, D.C., was a time of luxury and excess. Chic boutiques lined the streets and socialite types in minks stepped in and out of limos—it was winter, always winter. For two girls grounded in their Korean parents' humble beginnings in this country, the dripping wealth came close to culture shock.

Still, we'd done our homework and asked our architect to design a ritzy-glitzy sweetshop that captured the look of the day with Italian lighting, mirror-finish black marble floors, and three bubble-glassed candy cases. We were lucky enough to seal the deal on this location a stone's throw from the White House on Connecticut Avenue. Now our little no-name shop stood among Burberry and Cartier like Cinderella at the ball, a shop our late father would've loved just by virtue of its contents: chocolates and daughters. Were he alive, he could walk over from the World Bank during his lunch hour and visit us.

Yet were he alive, we would never have gone into business in the first place.

A few years earlier, Mom was accompanying Dad on a business trip to Bangkok that first included a personal stop to Seoul. Their itinerary, however, was cut short: En route, Dad suffered a fatal stroke in his sleep on the ninth floor of the Hyatt Regency Waikiki Hotel.

Back home, we were stunned. Lost. Dad was the one we looked up to. In a world where we grew up feeling we didn't quite belong, where even some of our neighbors made us feel unwelcome for being Asian, Dad's mere presence made us feel safe.

His World Bank colleagues always kidded him for settling his family down in middle-class Springfield instead of Great Falls and for driving a Gran Torino instead of a Mercedes-Benz. But Dad shunned lavish living on a globe where orphans still wandered and begged on the streets of postwar Seoul. He left their haunted faces behind, but sometimes the American way of life was a guilt trip for Dad. The truth was, he'd drive a jalopy as long as his family was with him.

That last night, had Dad known he would never wake up, he would never have fallen asleep.

While our siblings—older sister Grace and brother in between us Sam—remained close by, we grew Siamese. And while our natures were night and day—Francie dark, Ginger bright—without Dad, the only way we felt whole was to cling to each other, so cling we did, sister to sister until our souls were stitched tight. If we stuck together, somehow things would work out. Our grief was so deep only the promise to stick together and look after our widowed mother made us able to cope. Feel whole.

At the time, Francie, a published poet who couldn't stomach the New York literary scene, was halfheartedly working in an office at George Washington University. She was taking graduate courses in this and that and was dating a sweet pot-smoking professor. Because she didn't want to marry, Jim moved on—literally, to teach in Chicago. Ginger, who was attending a local college, had been infatuated with her guitar-strumming boyfriend Matt until she got the sense that he cared more about his guitar than her. Soon enough, she broke things off.

Suddenly, we were both single. Our destiny up for grabs.

Ginger lived at Mom's house with our moping Irish setter. Every night at seven o'clock sharp, Goldie would sit on the staircase by the front door and wait for Dad to come home from work. Francie rented an apartment closer to the city, though she was over half the time.

"Why not you save money and live here?" Mom would beg her. "Two empty bedroom."

"Sorry, Mom," she'd decline with a hug.

At twenty-four, Francie needed her own place, somewhere to steal away to if only for a moment and ponder the literary what-ifs of her life, even if her own current catchphrase was "It ain't happening now." She had Dad's death to recover from.

~~~

Chocolate was our comfort food, and we spent our days munching away on Hershey Kisses wondering whether we should go into business together, invest in a new life with the small inheritance Dad left us. Not really a far-fetched idea . . .

Once upon a time, we were Big Sis, Little Sis, celebrating every Christmas next to the fake silver tree our family dragged out of the attic year after year.

One particular holiday, the fireplace crackled and spat while Dad nursed his pipe and Mom puffed on her beloved Virginia Slims. Ginger was putting on an acrobatic show for the family, a razzle-dazzle routine of handstands, somersaults, and aerials. Between sips of sherry, our parents watched their youngest and nodded, whispering to each other in Korean. Sitting on the plaid couch in our wood-paneled rec room, sharing the stolen moment, they came together as almost the same person.

Christmas in our household had always been about singing Korean songs and eating hot chestnuts, not exchanging extravagant gifts. So Ginger couldn't believe her eyes when she tore the wrapping off a big red-and-gold-striped box and found that her wildest dream had come true: At six years old, she was the proud owner of an Easy-Bake Oven.

"I can't believe it!" She danced around the room.

"Sorry, Ginge, but you're too little to operate this thing by yourself," Francie observed.

Mom set up the oven on the yellow laminate kitchen counter to the right of the sink. There, facing a window that overlooked our backyard, we spent every morning of that Christmas vacation baking up a storm. The Easy-Bake Oven Shoppe was open for business! By noon, the whole house smelled of cake. When Dad came home from work, the lingering aroma, warm and homey, put him in a good mood.

"My little bakers have been busy!"

We were a true sister act, bickering, laughing, and licking our fingers, our entire focus that holiday on an oven whose heat source was a thumb-sized lightbulb. We burned through bulb after bulb, making miniature cakes from Easy-Bake kit mixes, turning them out so fast we could've opened up shop. The cake mixes came in several varieties, but one flavor ruled.

Chocolate.

When we ran out of the chocolate mixes, we had to think, think, think. How could we turn the white cakes into chocolate ones?

Francie clapped. "I got it."

We mixed a spoonful or two of cocoa into the white cake mix until the powder turned chocolate colored. Then we added water and stirred the brown batter into the two mini–cake pans. Breathless, we slid the pans into the Easy-Bake and peered through the glass window waiting for the moment the cakes began to puff higher and higher.

"Here it comes, Ginge."

"Wow . . ."

When the cakes were cooled, Ginger proved her wunderkind ways when it came to things chocolate.

"Get me down the Bosco!"

Grinning wickedly, she spooned the syrup all over the cooled cake. The frosting, though runny, was gorgeously chocolate, as was every black crumb on the counter.

So, could we stay Big Sis, Little Sis as business partners? Did we have the true enterprising spirit to make it work?

Dreams *were* possible. Our parents, who had survived harsh times in Korea under Japanese rule and the Korean War, were proof.

Dad, reared in a one-room mud hut with a family of eight, was blessed with a passport out of poverty: a gift for language. He worked his way to Harvard University and the World Bank until one day he bought the house of his dreams in suburban Virginia where he planted his gardens and built a life. Meanwhile, Mom, with an English all her own, staked her claim as boss of the Park home and, despite a childhood of being served meals by maids, learned to cook Korean feasts the neighbors could only dream of. That our parents came to America with nothing more than the clothes on their backs made us believe we too could do anything we set our minds to.

Since we were chocoholics long before it was a diagnosis, opening a sweet boutique felt like the most natural thing in the world. We began to dream of a store filled to the brim with chocolate, the smell of it wafting onto the street and luring in strangers. Maybe we'd even make friends. Build a business and a life, a rich life, around chocolate. Our shop would be our home away from home.

The only problem? We were two blind mice who didn't know what we were doing. After all, how on earth do you build a mythical chocolate castle? We couldn't even come up with a name.

Chocolate Heaven? No.

The Chocolate Bar? No, no.

A Chocolate Affair? No, no, no.

Aside from Mom, who planned to be our silent partner, most people thought we were out of our minds to go into business, especially when interest rates for bank certificates of deposit ranged from eighteen to twenty-one percent. You girls will *never* see that kind of return. How much chocolate can you *really* sell? Plus, you have no experience. Play it safe. Keep doing what you're doing.

We didn't listen. We had our calling.

Besides, we were sure we had Dad's blessing. In his lifetime, he fulfilled many dreams but not the Big One: to one day return to his war-torn homeland and help make a difference; perhaps even run for president. As a senior at Yonsei University, Dad had been appointed personal secretary to the country's first president-elect, Syngman Rhee; fluent in English, his role was to serve as a liaison between Korea and the United States. The Korean War would change everyone's fate, including his. During his years at Harvard grad school, the political climate in Korea turned more dangerous than ever, and he ended up not only postponing the dream but also resculpting his ambitions in America. He took much pleasure and contentment in life here. However, in 1979, the timing turned ripe, both politically and personally. Ginger was ready to graduate from high school and he was offered a cabinet position in Korea. Now he was ready to fly to Seoul to engage in discussions and hopefully live out his dream. Tragically, it was on that trip that he lost his life.

Yes, we had Dad's blessing every step of the way. And it wouldn't surprise him to know we were still thinking chocolate.

One day Ginger pulled a batch of brownies out of the oven to cool while Francie sat at the kitchen table at Mom's house—our designated "headquarters"—perusing wholesale catalogs mailed to us from San Francisco's Ghirardelli Chocolates and the Dutch maker Droste. We were trying to drum up a name for our shop to be. Think, damn it, think . . . The brownie aroma was too distracting.

Ginger sliced her sister a brownie nearly as big as the paper napkin it was served on. Francie's first bite was accompanied by an uninhibited groan of pleasure.

"Where'd you find this recipe? They're so chocolaty."

"No recipe." Ginger chewed. "I just added chocolate chips so they're twice as chocolaty. Double chocolate."

Francie licked crumbs, eyes dreamy, half closed. "Chocolate . . . chocolate . . ."

Ginger looked at her. "What'd you say?"

"I said—"

At that sister-to-sister moment, genius struck us.

"CHOCOLATE CHOCOLATE!"

We high-fived.

We hugged.

We did a silly dance.

Ginger sliced the rest of her brownies into mouth-popping bite-sized cubes. We popped away, starved.

"You know, you should think about making a signature piece of chocolate," Francie suggested. "Just one piece to put us on the map."

"Naw, too much pressure."

"I'd help."

"You're a ditz in the kitchen." Ginger coughed up crumbs. "You can't even sift flour."

Licking her fingers, Francie laughed. "True, so true."

Soon thereafter, we both quit doing what we were doing. No longer lost, we would road-map our lives together, with Mom at our side, of course. Dad, too, in spirit.

Chapter 2

Chocolate Apple

*A milk chocolate apple
that, when tapped,
falls into twenty perfect slices*

Dreaming about a chocolate shop and actually owning a chocolate shop were worlds apart. Without retail résumés—unless you counted Francie's summer job at Giant Music when she was more interested in the long-haired guys she worked with than selling records, or Ginger's shopaholic disorder—we definitely had our work cut out for us.

First step, research.

We ordered pamphlets from the Small Business Administration, poring over them like Bibles at Mom's kitchen table. Through the SBA we signed up for a course given by an organization of retired businesspeople who taught us the golden rule for success: location, location, location.

SBA certified, we began a full-time hunt for a location, combing through the *Washington Post* classifieds. Get your coffee, get your pen . . . Every morning brought new hope.

"Circle here." Francie pointed to a listing in Foggy Bottom. "It's a space on Red Lion Row at 2000 Pennsylvania Avenue, right near my old office. Lots of students there."

"Okay." Ginger circled. "Look, here's another space on Pennsylvania Avenue."

Francie frowned at the shady address. "Wrong end of Pennsylvania, Ginge. Look for NW, not SE." Ever the older sister.

Sunday listings were often three columns long, and Monday's business supplement was chock-full of possibilities. Our countless meetings with loudmouthed brokers and agents went nowhere except to educate us in the ways of small business leasing. Indeed, we got pretty fluent in lease lingo and could say "Go to hell" without flinching.

For months we drove around the metropolitan area and checked out empty storefronts, some we even liked. If Mom didn't come with us, she was headquartered at home, smoking Virginia Slims and playing *Yamagada*, Asian solitaire. When a Yamagada game got going, her deck of cards held all the answers to the universe, or at least whether we would find a good location that day.

"Any luck, girls?"

"Not today, Mom."

For not any old space would do. It had to be love.

Then it happened: We laid eyes on an Oz of a building where million-dollar marble met a soaring sun-gilded skylight, where the sidewalks out front were bustling, and gutsy notes from a live trumpet put a bounce in everyone's steps.

It was love at first sight.

And in our love-struck minds, the vacant lobby space on the corner, a space small and sparkly as a diamond, was ours, the perfect place for our chocolate castle. Close to the Farragut North Metro stop, with both street and lobby exposure, the lot was as prime as retail got in the downtown core where nearly every powerhouse D.C. law firm had set up practice, tailor-made for what was then just a lovely dream—Chocolate Chocolate.

Armed with a proposal, we called the landlord's leasing agent, who sounded like a fast-talking, cold-eyed shark. After revealing that while the landlord had slated this particular spot for an exclusive chocolatier, Jaws made it clear he was interested only in stores with international drawing power, not two local yokels reading SBA pamphlets. While our vision meant nothing to him, it was all we could see.

Already in town were several operations selling single-brand American candy such as Chez Chocolat and Fannie May. We, however, imagined taking Washingtonians on a more adventurous journey, offering a global range of chocolate from Zurich to Brussels to Baltimore to San Francisco. If other chocolate lovers were anything like us, sometimes you craved the private pleasure of a liqueur-laced European truffle and other times there was nothing better than chewing on an old-fashioned American vanilla caramel, horse-faced and all.

"Look," he said flatly, "Godiva's already leased that space."

In 1983, Godiva was the reigning designer chocolate company in the country, modeled after their Belgian namesake. Beautiful confections.

With a final snap, Jaws added, "Their sign's going up next week."
Click.

Heartbroken, we resumed our search. By car and on foot, we

hunted in vain for the second-best location we could find. Hearing much talk in the news about the revitalization of the area east of downtown as we knew it—around the F Street Corridor whose retail heyday ended with the Martin Luther King riots of 1968—we drove over. But other than department stores like Hecht's and Woodies and posh Garfinckel's where our older sister Grace was a fashion buyer, the empty retail spaces in between them were uninhabitable. Taped-up glass, trash on the street, broken beer bottles everywhere.

"Look at this place," Ginger cried, speeding through it.

"Accelerate!"

The zone might spring back to life someday, but not today.

Besides, our hearts really weren't in the search—second-best was a far cry—and we always ended back at the same spot with the same lament.

"*That's* where we belong."

A week passed and again we drove by the space, Ginger slowing down to a snail's pace. Francie shook her head, not wanting her heart broken yet another time.

"Why are we torturing ourselves? I don't want to see the Godiva sign."

"Hey," Ginger noted, "it's not up yet."

Francie nodded. "Interesting."

Another week passed. We drove by again, holding our breath.

"Hey," Ginger noted again, "still no Godiva sign."

"*Very* interesting."

One day, dying to know what was going on in there, we circled the block a half-dozen times looking for a metered parking space, to no avail.

"I'm double-parking," Ginger decided, braking across the street, "right here."

Then we dodged street traffic and peered into the space for clues. Empty.

"Should we call Jaws again?" Ginger said.

Francie's breath fogged up the glass. "What do we have to lose?"

Jaws couldn't hurt us, we decided, no matter how sharp he could be, especially with a telephone between us.

"Look, the Godiva deal fell through," he spat, probably wishing us minnows would swim away and never come back. "But I'm in negotiations with a Kron franchisee now and she's about to sign on the dotted line."

Kron, another big name in chocolate, was famous for their signature truffles and molds of chocolate body parts. We left our phone numbers with Jaws just in case Kron backed out, figuring he crumpled them up the minute we got off the phone. Reluctantly, we fell back into our routine, looking at other locations but still pining for the empty corner space in the beautiful marble building.

Our space.

Time passed with no sign of Kron moving in, and no new locations to love. Just as we contemplated calling Jaws again, the telephone rang at Mom's house. Francie, who was poring over the classifieds, answered it. On the phone was Ben, a mild-mannered attorney from the landlord's office, filling in for Jaws, who was on vacation. Francie motioned to Ginger, who picked up on the other line.

Fate must've been looking down on us, because Ben was about to begin a dialogue that would change the course of our lives.

"I have a note here that the Park sisters inquired about the vacant retail space at—"

Like magnets, our eyes locked. "Yes."

Hallelujah—the Kron deal had fallen through, too. We scheduled a meeting for the next day. Meetings were nothing new to us, but this one held the weight of the world and suddenly we were grateful to every sleazeball who tried to make a quick buck off of us. Now we were expert on the topics of rent and store build-out allowances.

We got ready for our meeting with Ben, putting on our makeup and rehearsing in the mirror what we would counteroffer with and ask for. Negotiate. Our women-of-the-world act might be hard to pull off in person, especially with Mom's cross-armed reflection watching us, but shoulder-to-shoulder sisterhood was always empowering, or at least we hoped.

"Ginge, what are you wearing?"

"My new black Tahari suit. Intimidating, don't you think?"

"Yeah, and so is Siren Red," Francie said, twisting up a tube of lipstick for show.

Meanwhile, Mom, waving a finger, had her own two cents to add. "You ask for building allowance. Twenty thousand dollar, not one penny less."

In the mirror, we both agreed. After all, our silent partner was the real boss.

Just before leaving, we checked each other out.

"Great dress," Francie said, grabbing scissors, "but maybe we should remove the price tag, Ginge."

Meanwhile, Francie's white blouse–black skirt ensemble met with Ginger's approval. "You look like a real power player."

Francie strutted her stuff. "It's the shoulder pads, baby."

By the time we got to the landlord's office, we were painted and padded and perfumed with Mom's Chanel. Still, Ben didn't attempt to hide his shock when he saw us.

"How old are you two?"

"In our twenties," we said.

His face flooded with doubt. "Okay . . ."

Meanwhile, we took the liberty of fanning out colorful catalogs of chocolates on his desk. His smile was controlled.

"I take it these are the lines you would carry?"

"The tip of the iceberg," Francie replied.

"Can't you almost *smell* the chocolate?" Ginger chipped in, retrieving a little box containing Droste's trademark Milk Chocolate Apple from her handbag.

"Yes," he had to admit, "I really can."

Ginger placed the blue-foiled apple on his desk, gave it a good tap, then removed the foil. To Ben's surprise, the apple fanned into twenty perfect chocolate slices.

"May I?" he asked, reaching for a slice.

"Of course."

"And," Francie got carried away, "our little pastry chef Ginger will be unveiling her very own chocolat de vie on opening day!"

"I must say," Ben said, unaware of the kick Little Sis just gave Big Sis under the desk, "my mouth is watering."

When we presented Ben with our financial statement, any second thoughts he had flew out the window. Even in death, Dad took care of us. Having grown up in Korea so impoverished he weighed less than a hundred pounds on his wedding day, he vowed his wife and kids would never know a day of money worries, much less hunger. Our family lived modestly while he saved wisely. With the inheritance he left us, combined with Mom's finances, our portfolio was quite impressive.

When Ben told us how much the rent was, however, we swallowed hard, pinching each other under the desk. The number was twice as high as the going rate for a small space in the neighborhood. On the spot, we propped each other up and counteroffered with forty dollars less per square foot.

"And," Francie again spoke up, "we also require a twenty-thousand-dollar building allowance."

"You *what?*"

"It'll cost a pretty penny to build out this shop, and we can't foot the whole bill," Ginger explained in a brave if not well-rehearsed way. "Twenty thousand dollars, and that's our final offer."

Miraculously, and without consulting the landlord, Ben accepted both terms of our offer, proving that they were as desperate to fill the space *now* as we were to be there. No one was going to be a fool about it. Over the next few days we hammered out minor lease details, and when the final contract was delivered to our headquarters via Federal Express, we three signed on the dotted lines. Then Mom opened a jug of Gallo Chablis for her and Francie, and a bottle of iced tea for Ginger, the teetotaler.

"Big day!" Mom cheered.

Next step: Hire an architect.

Mitchell Mirage was like walking lung cancer—he could never get a sentence out without a major coughing fit. There were times we wondered whether he'd even be around long enough to see our project to fruition. His gruff sincerity, along with his reputation, assured us of his talents.

"The space is small," he said, coughing up a storm at the conference table in his office that overlooked the C&O Canal, "a shoe box considering your plans for it. But I love a challenge."

Mitchell was used to designing thematic malls and swanky restaurants with spiral staircases, not shoe box boutiques. But somehow, in between smoke breaks, he found a way to put our vision on paper, even abiding by all government rules, regulations, and red tape. His sketches and blueprints wowed us, and the idea that these images would soon transfer to real life was almost too much to compute.

Along with the shiny black marble floor and walls and Italian lighting, the drawings called for tiny track lights over our candy cases that would reflect off chrome shelves, creating a diamondlike light effect. The back room would house all the sinks required for a candy store: a three-compartment sink, a hand sink, and a mop sink, with just enough room left over to have a slow dance, if there was anyone to slow-dance with.

One day in the spring of 1983, a day of limbo, of waiting for the landlord to approve the blueprints, we cruised downtown for no other reason than simply to stare at the space—*our* space.

Washington, blessed with the Potomac River and the country's most imposing architecture, is a breathtaking city every season of the year. But spring takes the cake. Picture the Capitol Dome and the Tidal Basin, the Smithsonian Castle and the Washington Monument, flanked with yearning daffodils, tulips, and magnolias, sunlight playing off every surface.

Cherry Blossom season was in full swing as we crossed Arlington Memorial Bridge and around the Lincoln Memorial with Ginger at the wheel as usual—she'd rather drive than twiddle her thumbs any old day. The boisterous part of her wanted to roll down her window and shout, "We're home, Washington!" but that wasn't her sister's speed. Lately Francie preferred low-keyed living, peace and quiet. Between us, we'd never have to utter a word, so completely at ease with each other as we were, a level of comfort dating back to our childhood walks up to Safeway or 7-Eleven for treats: Big Sis, Little Sis.

This scenic part of town—with tourists, trolleys, and flowering trees—filled us with near awe. Although our family had lived in the area since 1960, our hometown in suburban Virginia was seventeen miles and light-years down I-395. It was more like Mayberry, and we were probably less worldly than we would have liked to admit.

As we turned onto Constitution Avenue, rain began to fall and umbrellas mushroomed on a path winding through the new Vietnam Veterans Memorial. The rain picked up and every so often pinkish petals scattered across the windshield. After turning left on 18th Street, we passed Foggy Bottom, home to George Washington University and the World Bank, staring up at 717 18th Street as if Dad might be looking down on us from his office window on the seventh floor. Was it really possible he'd been gone nearly four years? *Four years.* Then again, sometimes it felt longer . . . We crossed Pennsylvania Avenue and through a corridor of buildings and red and yellow awnings, turned right, until there it was, our destination. Our Oz.

"We're home, Francie."

"I know."

With its soaring glass atrium, Oz crowned an intersection regarded as D.C.'s version of Times Square, minus the grittiness. Yes, downtown Washington was free of grime, but what truly made the city shine that day, at least in our eyes, was a temporary sign posted on a wooden barricade: COMING SOON, CHOCOLATE CHOCOLATE. In a crowded lunch-hour lobby of workers coming and going, Ginger took Francie's arm.

"Listen."

Two people were chanting, "Chocolate Chocolate," followed by more of the same.

"Chocolate Chocolate, Chocolate Chocolate, Chocolate Chocolate . . ."

It was a chant that echoed all our years of dreaming. The kind of moment you don't have every day. Like pouring liquid chocolate into a mold, our dream was beginning to take shape.

Chapter 3

Burgundy Grappe

Chocolate-burgundy cream
piped into a bittersweet grape cluster

Starting our own business was beginning to feel like a piece of cake—or, better yet, a blissful chocolate mint, one with snap and linger. We had come up with the stand-out name, found an elegant space, been approved by the landlord, and hired an architect. Everything was going our way, and we broke into song whenever Madonna came over the car radio, singing *"Holiday . . . Celebrate . . ."*

But before we could celebrate, there was much work to do.

Next step: Find a general contractor. Our architect recommended Sonny Campbell. Sonny *who?* While not experts when it came to general contractors, we'd been around the block, literally, during our search for a space. Massive signs advertising the same industry names were staked in grounds all over D.C. construction sites. They were the who's who of local general contractors, and Sonny Campbell wasn't among them.

"He was the supervisor on my last job in Washington, and he did an excellent job," Mitchell informed us at his office, no sooner crushing out a cigarette than lighting up another. "He used to work for Charles Kitt Associates, and for a Dallas contractor before that, but he recently started his own company, Campbell Construction. Like all new guys, he's desperate for work. Eager, I mean."

Ginger cast doubt. "You sure his name isn't Sonny *Gamble?*"

"Look," he said, "when you're a little fish in a big sea, small jobs like yours mean more. He'll give you the personal attention the bigger contractors won't, and charge you a hell of a lot less, too. Just meet with him and see how you feel."

"We still want three bids," Francie insisted.

Mitchell nodded. "Fair enough."

Mitchell set up our meeting at Vie de France, a café-bakery footsteps from Oz on K Street. We'd already met with two other contractors who fit the bill, but neither particularly impressed us. One was a half hour late and the other kept checking his beeper even when it wasn't beeping. On the other hand, Sonny Campbell was more than prompt—he was eagerly waiting for us with Mitchell outside the café. And in the looks department, he was quite a departure from the other two, presenting a clean-cut image in a crisp blue blazer over jeans and a white shirt.

Mitchell introduced us. "Meet Francie and Ginger, the proprietors of the soon-to-be-built Chocolate Chocolate."

With a deep drawl, Sonny said, "God bless your parents—it's a pleasure to meet two such lovely sisters."

Inside Vie de France, a lunch spread was already set out for us at a table by the window—baguette sandwiches, fruit tarts, iced tea. As if we were dining at Dominique's, Sonny held our chairs open.

"So," he began, "what can I do to convince you that I'm the man for the job?"

Ginger was frank. "You could start with a low bid."

"Ginger," Mitchell wheezed, "I just gave him the plans yesterday."

"I'll have a bid to you by the end of the week," Sonny promised, looking each of us in the eye.

"A list of references would help, too," Francie added, noting his bright blue eyes. "What other projects have you done?"

"Look around town," Sonny said with a wave of his hand. "I've worked on many of these buildings as a supervisor for Charles Kitt Associates, but Chocolate Chocolate would be my first project under Campbell Construction."

Our uncomfortable silence prompted his plea. "And I swear I'd give it my all."

"So," Francie asked, sipping her iced tea, "why'd you decide to go into business for yourself?"

"I've been working for someone else my whole life, Francie. At forty-eight"—he paused—"I decided it's my time to live out my dream."

Ginger nearly choked on her baguette. "You're forty-eight?"

"Ginger," Sonny said with a smile, "I certainly hope that's a compliment."

Mitchell elbowed his friend. "That makes us the same age."

Poor Mitchell. If smoking wasn't the death of him, it surely was the aging of him.

"Francie and Ginger," Sonny stated for the record, "when I say I want this job more than my competition does, I mean it. As you both know, everyone's got to start somewhere, right?"

Back at the shop, Francie remarked, "Cute."

"And can you believe he's forty-eight?"

"He's got some serious schoolboy charm going on."

"A little *too* charming but I like him . . . I think."

"Me, too . . . I think."

He had said everyone's got to start somewhere. Couldn't we re-late? Maybe taking a gamble with Sonny Campbell was the way to go, assuming he came in with the lowest bid.

He did. Campbell Construction's was twenty-three thousand dollars lower than the closest bidder. Our decision was made for us.

In the meantime, we had a store to stock.

Our domestic offerings were already lined up. From the minute our name appeared on the barricade, local candy reps were all over us, and by now we'd met with more of them than we could remem-ber in the Connecticut Connection, an underground eatery in a neighboring building. There, on tiny tables, reps presented us with confections whose fragrance competed with the smell of greasy french fries and pizza.

One meeting was particularly memorable. The rep set out a dozen brick-sized candy bars, each one topped with chocolate shav-ings, colorful jimmies, or shredded coconut.

"Wow," was all we could say.

The group at the table next to us watched and drooled.

"Need some help?" one guy offered.

"Trade you my lunch for yours," his colleague joked.

But these, like most samples, were disappointing—stale, cloy-ingly sweet, or made of "mock chocolate," that is, more filler than cocoa beans. Too polite to say they sucked, Francie simply shrugged: "Sorry."

All we wanted were the highest-quality chocolates on the Amer-ican map from nostalgic nougats and turtles to nouveau truffles. Filling the bill of chocolates for every mood meant a wide variety and price range, yet it all had to taste good. No, *great*. In the end, on the home front we picked our favorites.

First off, Candy Jar truffles from San Francisco. Unlike many imitators, these were the real deal in what was then the debut of truly gourmet chocolate manufactured in the USA. As premiere as any fine European line, they were, however, rather humongous, eschewing delicacy for whimsy. The chocolate maestro was a Hungarian woman named Maria who loved to talk on the phone while orchestrating her candy kitchen. With the help of her daughter Carla, each truffle center was hand-dipped in milk, dark, or white chocolate, then topped off with a sprinkle of, say, macadamia nuts or almond slivers or dried fruit. Each flavor garnered its own signature chocolate flourish, with some showered in cocoa powder.

Second, Asher's Chocolates from Philadelphia, whose homemade appeal came from the original recipes founder Chester Asher wrote on the back of sugar bags in the late 1800s. Their chocolate pretzels cracked with a salty sweetness that made you reach for one after another . . .

Third, Naron Candies from Baltimore. Naron made some of the best old-fashioned chocolates in the country. Peanut Butteries so smooth you could spread them on bread. Milk Pecan Turtles that boasted the best of both worlds—crunch *and* chew. Clusters, Almond Butter Crisps, Heavenly Hash bars. Who could resist? Not us.

Now the time had come to see what the world of imported chocolates had to offer us. On a Friday in early summer 1983, we took a train up to New York City to attend the International Summer Fancy Food and Confection Show. According to our American vendors, the show was supposedly the World's Fair of gastronomical pleasures.

～～

We stepped off the train at Penn Station lugging suitcases over-stuffed with electric hair rollers, shoes, magazines, makeup, and way too many outfits for one weekend. Our big bags and eager eyes were dead giveaways that we weren't native New Yorkers. Out of nowhere a smiling man approached us. A Penn Station porter, we presumed, offering to carry our suitcases to the taxi stand. May I? Sure! Those bags were back-breaking. Francie, in her high-heeled sandals, was especially pleased. You couldn't pay her to wear sensible shoes.

The man took our bags and began walking ahead of us.

Whoever said New Yorkers were rude? What a great city! Wait—why was he walking so fast? Through the crowd, we took turns calling out to him.

"Slow down!"

Instead, he sped up.

"He's stealing our stuff!"

As he exited Penn Station and hoofed his way down Seventh Avenue, we chased after him, weaving through the crowds of people. Our presumed porter was a thug and trying his best to lose us. Francie called out, knowing she couldn't run another step in those shoes.

"Drop the bags!"

In Washington, people took note when a young woman screamed; at the very least, they'd call the police. But in New York, this was just another day. Slowing with defeat, she sicced her sister on him.

"Go get him, Ginge!"

Ginger, ever the athlete in Nikes and 1980s spandex, stepped up her pursuit. Her normally sweet countenance had morphed into rage—no one was getting away with this! Our heavy suitcases turned out to be a blessing; soon his arms tired and his pace slowed while she closed the gap, practically in vault position.

"Drop those bags!" she cried at the top of her lungs.

Ginger's ferocity stunned him; he dropped our bags without turning around and disappeared down 31st Street.

"And stay away from us, you SOB!"

Instead of hailing a cab, we held on to our suitcases very, very tightly and hobbled over to the InterContinental hotel a few blocks away.

On Saturday we made our way to the exhibition hall. The buzz was electric. Thousands of purveyors from all over the globe had set up booths to showcase everything the gourmet food industry had to offer retailers. From gelato to crepes to fois gras and caviar, we wanted to sample it all, but we planned to save our appetites for the food of the gods: chocolate.

At the registration booth we presented the lively check-in lady with the proper credentials. In turn, she handed us badges that displayed our names as well as our shop name and address. As far as we were concerned, these were badges of honor and we pinned them on like medals, gleaming.

We were off to the candy races.

Like kids at 7-Eleven again grabbing Tootsie Pops and Snickers bars, we sampled our way through the confection aisles until falling into a chocolate coma. Definition of cloud nine: being surrounded by more chocolate than you could eat in a lifetime.

Deep into the trade show scene, aggressive chocolate makers and their reps serenaded retailers. The most entertaining reps were foreign, trying to usher their imported chocolates into American shops. At first we were worried no one would take us seriously, but to our delight, we were instantly circled by reps showering us with compliments, samples, and sweet talk.

"So you darling girls are going into business in Washington, D.C.?" asked a rep named Josephine from the Chocolat de Paris booth, eying our badges and signaling someone over. "You will make a fortune your first year."

"Bonjour," her colleague greeted us. "I am Signe, the U.S. manager, at your service."

"Nice to meet you," we said, sampling their wares.

Their line tasted high quality but somewhat chalky with a distinct sour after-note. Our exchanged twitch confirmed that this was not for us. We tried to slip away, only to find ourselves circled by Chocolat de Paris reps holding order forms.

"Where exactly on Connecticut Avenue will your shop be? Near the White House?" Signe wondered.

"A few blocks away," we said.

"President Reagan is wild about Jelly Bellies, you know."

"Yes, we heard . . ."

"What shiny hair you girls have," remarked Josephine.

"Thank you . . ."

"You'll have the men in Washington eating chocolates out of your hands."

When a matronly woman in a gold brocade suit—the grande dame of Chocolat de Paris, perhaps?—came wobbling over, we took our cue and broke away from the circle.

"We'll be back," Francie said.

"We promise," Ginger said.

We scurried away and snaked through the crowd, accidentally bumping into other attendees until a booth flanked with mini Italian flags slowed us down: Perugina Chocolates, famous in New York for their flagship store on Lexington Avenue. A raven-haired beauty approached us with a tray of silver- and blue-foiled bonbons.

"Try a Baci. It is singly the most famous piece of chocolate in the world. Look at it. Not only is it so beautiful and delicious, there is a precious little poem inside, a little fortune. But taste, taste— you will go crazy for it, I guarantee you."

Our introduction to Baci lived up to the Perugina rep's description. There was something alluring about the whole romantic package, not to mention the sensation of crunch against velvet chocolate, an almost erotic light-headedness. Rosa made quite an impression when she slipped each of us a blue velvet sachet filled with Baci kisses. Perugina chocolates were definitely in our future.

Not every experience was so elevating. Belgian chocolates were also on our sumptuous list of things to check out. Two major importers, Neuhaus of Brussels and Maison d'Or, were in the running. Since both were touted as the quintessential Belgian chocolate, our plan was to sample both and decide which one to stock in our shop.

We approached the Maison d'Or booth, ready to talk business. Unfortunately, the feeling wasn't mutual. A middle-aged woman with ample cleavage took one look at us and sniffed. Her somewhat younger male associate sheepishly followed suit—guess he left his balls in Belgium.

"No," she dismissed us, "we don't sell to your kind of store."

Our kind of store? And exactly what kind of store did she think we had? She hadn't even bothered to look at our badges.

"Our shop is going to be in the heart of downtown Washington, D.C.," Francie said, growing scarlet.

"We sell only to exclusive shops," the rep said. As she turned her cheek, Francie caught a whiff of perfume that nearly knocked her over. The rep quickly busied herself by straightening up a stack of brochures while her associate cowered in the background.

Ginger, hands on hips, made a prediction. "One day you'll eat your words, madame."

Thankfully, the red carpet was rolled out for us at the Neuhaus of Brussels booth, where their display cases featured tray after tray of confections almost too lovely to eat, with names to match—Fruits de Mer, Cornet Doré, Sapho, Coquille—in stunning contrast to a row of earthy-looking truffles. Things were hopping here, and in the midst of all the activity, one of their reps, an eager New Yorker named Elizabeth, spoiled us with Belgian specialties including hazelnut nougats and cognac truffles and pistachio marzipan. Basically, everything a chocoholic could wish for.

"So, girls, did ya die and go to heaven?"

To put it mildly, yes.

Meanwhile, Ginger had her eye on one more praline, as Europeans refer to all chocolates—a grape-cluster-sculpted piece polished onyx black. "It looks like it belongs in a museum," she noted.

"I know, I know," Elizabeth agreed. "But I tell you, once you try it, you'll never be the same. It's called a Grappe."

With silver tongs, Elizabeth, as if handling the Hope Diamond, placed a single Grappe in Ginger's palm. Ginger picked it up, felt it.

"It's smooth as stone."

Once she cracked into its shell, a gush of intense bittersweet chocolate and burgundy cream made her sigh as if her whole soul had been coated in chocolate.

"I'm going to remember this, Francie, for the rest of my life."

This was true.

Their chocolates, we would learn, were as rich as their history. Established in 1857, rumor had it that Neuhaus still used old world methods as well as the original antique chocolate molds. Royalty in Belgium, they were little known in America and anxious for a presence in the nation's capital. When Elizabeth introduced us to a circle of higher-ups in suits, everyone shook hands, and history was made.

Our Belgian line chosen, now it was time to find a Swiss coun-
terpart. In the 1980s, Teuscher of Switzerland, with two shops in
Manhattan and a reputation for sterling champagne truffles, was
the choice for those with refined chocolate palates. Weeks earlier,
we had written a letter of inquiry to the company headquarters in
Zurich, only to be informed that they didn't wholesale to outsiders.
Despite this setback, we knew that Swiss chocolate's international
reputation was well-founded. If we couldn't have Teuscher, we
would find another line, just as good or better. We vowed to, in
memory of Dad.

Dad's work took him overseas and he was gone half the time, helping people in poverty-stricken nations. His heart went out to them
and never quite let go, evidenced by all the stories and pictures he
came back with: stick-thin brown children from El Salvador, Mad-
agascar, Gabon, all over the map.

Ginger would sleep with his picture under her pillow, for he—
who always tucked her in—seemed so far away he might never
come back. She missed tagging along on his walks with Goldie
around the neighborhood, which was much more fun than being
his garden gofer. Still, when he was away, she would miss that, too.
Francie would yearn for their roundtable talks in the living room,
long after dinner, when he would try to enlighten her by talking
about Tolstoy and Gandhi and ancient philosophers whose ridiculously long names she could never remember. His talks were all
wrapped up around greatness and how he wished it upon all his
children, though he saw us in star-struck lights: Francie, the next
Madame Curie; Ginger, the next Olga Korbut.

"I'll be home soon, kids," he always said.

And so in his beloved green-shuttered house swept with silence, we'd wander from room to room awaiting his return, crossing paths with Goldie until seven o'clock when she could be found on the staircase, waiting for him. Long-distance phone calls were prohibitive and his airmail letters and postcards took at least a week to get to us—proof that Dad was continents away. We felt every mile of separation, the total disconnect. His echo haunted us.

"I'll be home soon, kids."

Needless to say, his homecomings were always a big deal. Since Mom didn't drive, he had to catch a cab from Dulles Airport. At the door he'd be greeted with a big WELCOME HOME! banner over the kitchen entry, the aroma of Korean food, and four kids flinging themselves into his arms.

Dad always returned from his trips bearing gifts, and our home was a veritable museum decorated with hand-carved elephants, African masks, exotic wall plates, and a collection of native dolls. One night, back from yet another foreign land, Dad unlatched his suitcase with a pirate flourish.

"Look inside, kids."

We blinked with disbelief at the vision of sleek candy bars— row after row, buried like treasure. With their blue-and-white scenic wrappers of the Alps and fair-haired milkmaids, these were no ordinary candy bars. These were the famous confections from Switzerland's Lindt Chocolatier.

Giddy, Ginger grabbed a bar, discarding the wrapper in record time. Then the two of us painstakingly broke it into little pieces along its scores onto a napkin before devouring them. Even as kids we could tell that this chocolate was unlike any other chocolate we'd had before.

"It tastes different," Francie said.

Ginger smacked her lips. "So*oooo* good."

So good, as if the milk from Swiss cows grazing on Swiss farms was creamier. In fact, each bite was so buttery good we could almost taste another land where chocolate came from fields, not factories.

Our memories of how happy Dad was to be home would linger in our minds for many years, along with a fondness for Swiss chocolate. But not long after our beaming dad presented us with a suitcase full of Lindt chocolate bars, we made a shocking discovery. On days when we both had the time and some extra pocket money, we loved to walk up to Safeway after school. There, browsing the aisles, something caught Francie's eye. Her gasp was so loud it almost knocked over the nearby Crisco cans. Neither of us had ever noticed the rack of Lindt bars before, but here they were, in the international aisle.

That night, we whispered in the dark, taking an oath of silence: "We'll never tell him."

The existence of the Lindt bars in Safeway would be our secret—forever.

So Sunday, our last day at the show, was dedicated to finding an exquisite Swiss line to round out our shop. The Altdorf of Switzerland booth was tucked away far from the madding candy crowds, on the lower level where it was suspiciously quiet. Two men were manning a candy case that housed an array of marble-sized truffles pyramided on gold trays. With a stall absent of any customers, we couldn't help but feel sorry for them. The elder man was seated, his cane nearby. The younger man, fair-haired and stocky in an ill-fitting suit, greeted us with enthusiasm.

"Hello, young ladies. My name is Peter and this is my father, Mr. Emminger."

The father seemed to speak no English but he greeted us with a gracious nod.

"Hello." We waved.

After exchanging cordialities, we explained what we were looking for. Peter explained that he and his father manufactured delicate truffles in the village of Altdorf located high in the Swiss Alps. They made them in very small batches that kept them milky and rich. To us, it sounded like the stuff of fairy tales.

"We have never exported our chocolates before," he admitted, "and we are here to see if there is any American interest. Are you interested?"

"Well"—we both grinned—"we have to try them first, don't we?"

The thing about chocolate is that no matter how much you've gorged the day before, you're always ready for more.

First up was a champagne truffle, dusted in powdered sugar. Like all their truffles, it sat atop a mound of truffles perfectly set; removing one might be risky.

"Looks like snowcaps in the Alps," Francie said, taking a bite. But the truffle tasted like something above the snowcaps—heaven. "Oh, my God, Ginge. You've got to try this."

Think marbled dark and white chocolate whipped with butter and fresh cream, splashed with champagne, then dipped in milk chocolate for a crunchy outer layer. If we sold nothing but these fragile beauties in our shop, we'd be rich. The next few bites, however, proved that their sugar-crystal raspberry and buttery white truffles were just as divine, lighter and fluffier than the densely decadent Neuhaus chocolates.

Sometimes sisters don't need to consult; we knew we were both in. So what if the Emmingers were inexperienced? We were novices, too.

"This is most exciting," Peter said breathlessly before conveying the good news to his father in German.

While Peter gathered the paperwork for us to fill out, Mr. Emminger hobbled over to us and shook our hands with gratitude.

"Thank you, thank you . . ."

Then, in a symbolic gesture, he presented us with a tray of little Swiss chocolate bars wrapped in shiny gold foil.

"Ingot." He smiled.

That night, on the train home, we shared a communal sigh and sank into our seats. Already our weekend at the International Summer Fancy Food and Confection Show took on a surreal glow. Did we really talk shop with veteran candy reps and place orders? Did it all really happen?

Francie reached into her show bag and pulled out her velvet Baci sachet. Proof we were there.

Our private party began with unwrapping and popping Bacis like popcorn and reliving the highlights of the show in whispers—the train was so quiet. We couldn't wait to share all the stories with Mom, home tonight playing cards and asking the Yamagada gods: *My daughters will come home safely from trip?* The truth was, Mom preferred to live through our adventures from the safety net of her own home where no one questioned her heavy accent. Her own adventures had exhausted her—the Korean War and the death of her husband. Often we tried to get her out, to no avail.

"I had a blast," Ginger said.

"Me, too."

Our incredible experience at the show—our star treatment—wasn't something we took for granted. Ginger suddenly hiccupped with laughter.

"Wasn't that funny when we made our great escape from the Chocolat de Paris booth?"

"Yeah, but I don't think that one lady thought so."

"What lady?"

Francie reminded her sister that in their getaway, they'd accidentally knocked into a short lady with fluffy silver-blond hair who looked to be bickering with a grumpy old man while fanning herself.

"Oh, right, the Little General!"

"This isn't a slumber party, girls," Francie said, doing a throaty imitation. Gobbling down another Baci, she added, "Guess we'll never see her again."

"Or that witch from Maison d'Or."

"More like Madame Skunk, considering her stinky perfume."

By now we were so drowsy and drunk on Bacis we broke out laughing until our eyes teared.

"Know something, Ginge?"

"What?"

"We'll never, ever treat our customers the way Madame Skunk treated us."

"Never."

The hour grew late; the train hushed as if talking was no longer allowed. Not that we needed to talk anymore; our minds were running on the same track and train of thought: Here we were, carrying back hopes and dreams for Chocolate Chocolate, carrying them like prized souvenirs packed in our hearts. We'd come so far from simply talking about the possibility of starting our own business. Now we were convinced: Our destination lay together—and Dad would be so proud.

Chapter 4

Half-Moon
Buttercream Dream

*A precious half-moon of milk
chocolate buttercream*

The morning after our return from the New York show, we were on an emotional high. Having made so many decisions about what would go *in* the store, we needed to make sure there would be a store to put them in. Up early and brimming with energy, we went to check up on our space to see how far along construction was. Inching up to the barricade, pressing our ears to the wood, we listened for the sounds of progress, that lovely symphony of saws and drills and hammers. Silence.

"Where is everyone?" we wondered.

This seemed like a rotten sign.

Sonny Campbell had promised to build out the most stunning

store in the city within six months and get us open in time for Christmas. Maybe we should've asked *which* Christmas.

Nearly a month ago at contract signing Sonny had required a check in the amount of forty thousand dollars as a down payment for his services, a small fortune in those days. Needless to say, we had a hard time parting with our check.

Francie was brooding. "Exactly what services are we paying you for?"

Ginger crossed her arms, deadpan. "That's an obscene amount of money."

Sonny had sighed. "I know, ladies, it sounds like beaucoup bucks, doesn't it? But it's just the way things work in the industry. Go through the Yellow Pages and call up any contractor, they'll tell you this is standard policy. Subcontractors won't step foot in here unless they're paid up front for their work. Bottom line, they don't want to be screwed. I mean, if a customer special-ordered five hundred wedding chocolates, you'd expect a deposit, wouldn't you? When you think about it, it's the same thing." He winked.

"Hmmm . . ." We wondered what wedding chocolates would cost forty grand.

"Francie, Ginger, think about the beautiful store you'll have. The most beautiful girls in the most beautiful store in town, you can't even pin a price on that—"

He didn't have to finish his sentence before the check was in his hands.

Now, from the pay phone in the building's garage, we were freaking out. Blind with rage, Francie couldn't even see straight enough to drop the dime in the slot. Ginger was cursing.

"Bullshitter!"

Sonny tried to calm us down, explaining that there were delays

due to obtaining various building permits and coordinating subcontractors.

"Don't you worry; we've got time to build *five* stores. The materials have all been ordered—glass, marble, millwork, chrome. Those
fancy lights from Italy are en route. We've got electricians and me-
chanical engineers lined up and ready to come in anytime. And
keep in mind that things are getting done behind the scenes in
warehouses and factories."

"Really?"

"You bet. The storefront sign's already made and sitting in a
warehouse, waiting to be installed. The thing to understand, ladies,
is that once we get all the pieces ready, the actual construction
only takes four or five weeks."

So, according to Sonny Campbell, the symphony of saws and
drills and hammers was going on behind closed doors, somewhere
over the rainbow. Did we believe him? To avoid nervous break-
downs, we tried.

What else could we do? Still, it was difficult to keep from worry-
ing with the constant reminder that we would soon be opening up
shop: Once word got out in the industry that a new chocolate shop
was opening in town, not a day went by without yet another ven-
dor calling to beg for an appointment. Most were from companies
that either couldn't afford to set up booths at the Fancy Food
Show, or were just getting off the ground. Poor timing, as we'd already ordered enough chocolate to stock our store, and there was
little room in our shop or our hearts to fall in love with any new
chocolates. One caller, however, was so persistent you could almost
see her shoe in the door.

"Ten minutes of your time, that's all I ask. You'll fall in love with
my chocolates, I'd bank my life on it."

We had agreed to meet Stella Rose, a rep for Babe's of San Francisco chocolates, at one o'clock in the Connecticut Connection, a couple of hours before our scheduled meeting with Sonny Campbell at Vie de France.

In a sea of workers eating lunch, we spied a handsome little woman with silver-blond puffs of hair and cat eyeglasses at a table near the cookie booth. We had a hunch that this was Stella. Fanning herself with a cardboard scrap, she looked strangely familiar.

"Stella?" Francie said.

Her hello was husky, almost stern. "Have a seat, girls. Don't mind my hot flash."

Ginger settled in. "Where have we seen you before?"

"Do you live in Rockville, Maryland?"

"No."

"I thought maybe we belonged to the same synagogue," she joked, still fanning.

"Stella . . . ," Francie began.

"Scoot closer, darling, I won't bite."

"Were you at the Fancy Food Show?"

"Yes, and my feet are still killing me. I feel like Debbie Reynolds after *Singin' in the Rain.*"

Aha! We instantly recognized her. "Why, you're the Little General," we said, laughing.

"I'm who? What?"

After good-naturedly pointing out that she had scolded us at the show, Ginger added, "It seemed like you and some man were having an argument."

Stella's fluffy head disagreed. "An old schlep in the industry stopping by the booth to catch up. Compared to usual, we were making love."

Somehow we had missed Babe's booth but registered seeing Stella.

"And we covered every inch of the show, twice," Francie was saying, "but never noticed your booth."

"Well, that's what happens when you split a booth four ways with four different vendors—you barely get an inch. Babe's is so cheap I had to pay my own way. Their idea of a fair per diem couldn't buy me a Slim Jim for lunch. But I wouldn't miss a show, not for anything in the world, though someone should tell them to turn up the air-conditioning."

Stella explained that Babe's had been churning out old-time favorites in hot pink hatboxes printed with black silhouettes of tea-drinking ladies since the 1890s. Watching our reactions, she slowly caressed the top of a box, then removed it with a flourish, revealing a mosaic of white-cupped confections from a bygone era, mostly pastel pink, white, and green squares topped with fleur-de-lis designs. Wedged in were a few half-moons of milk and dark chocolate, the only edible-looking ones. Francie was curious.

"What are those?"

"Half-Moon Buttercream Dreams. They're marvelous."

"What's the center like? Is it real sweet or—"

"Marvelous, they're all marvelous," Stella stated loudly, wide-eyed. "I worked at Woodies for seven years, and this line sold like hotcakes. My kids are so crazy about them I have to hide them or I won't have any samples for my clients. Try this one," she said to Ginger, holding up a pink square that matched her fake fingernails. "It's called a Dainty Lady and it's divine."

A nibble later, Ginger made a face. "It's so sweet my teeth hurt."

Stella chuckled, unconcerned by her reaction. "To each her own."

"Do you actually *eat* chocolate, Stella?"

"Not as much as I'd like to, Ginger—the tummy, don't you know.

Chocolate can be iffy, but seeds are my true nemesis. A single rai-sin can put me out for days."

"I think I'll try one of those half-moons," Francie said.

"You should. They're to die for."

Small and plain, no one would've asked to try these half-moons at the Fancy Food Show. But Francie dug one out of the box and took a brave bite anyway.

Imagine a little moon of chocolate, simple and smooth, even virtuous. A moon slowly melting onto your tongue, and every muscle instinctively melting with it. Imagine feeling so sated noth-ing could disappoint you ever again. That was the promise of a Half-Moon Buttercream Dream.

"Ginge, try one."

Instead, Ginger put two half-moons together, one milk, one dark, and slurped them up.

"Eh."

"What's in the red bag down there?" Francie inquired. "More samples?"

"No, darling, shoes. Three pairs. Every hour I rotate styles. You'll know what I mean when you're my age and your feet wage war on you."

"Okay."

Though Francie fell in love with Babe's Half-Moon Butter-cream Dreams, we couldn't do business with Stella for just one little piece; the minimum opening order was a thousand dollars, and by the time we sold a thousand dollars' worth of Half-Moon Buttercream Dreams, they'd be rocks, not creams.

"Not to worry," Stella said, packing up her chocolate. "I wish you two all the luck in the world with your new store."

We shared the hope to see Stella again, and said so.

"Oh, I'm not going anywhere," she retorted, squeezing our hands so tight her warmth seared us. "Have you girls had lunch yet?"

Afterward, we met Sonny Campbell at Vie de France, and once again, treats were awaiting us—this time, coffee and chocolate croissants.

"Eat up," Sonny insisted.

"We just ate," Francie said.

His crestfallen face made us feel bad, so we indulged, a little. A bite, a sip. Meanwhile, Sonny did his best to calm us down with progress reports detailing where every dollar was going. See? See? He was much more reassuring in person than on the phone. Another bite, another sip—okay, we felt a bit better. What did we know about the construction business, anyway? Still, our frustration was understandable when not a single nail had been hammered.

"I don't get it," Francie said.

"It's taking so long," Ginger complained.

"Look, I love you both, but some things are out of my hands. If it were up to me, I'd have started the day we met, but the government's modus operandi is to make our life hell. Mark my word, once we get the green light, I'm there, twenty-four/seven. I'm a hands-on guy."

But our hope waned when, day after day, we saw no progress in the shop. Exasperated, we threw up our hands. What could we do? Our trips downtown had become a waste of time; the hole behind the barricade was silent and black.

"If Dad were here to help us," Ginger kept wishing, "what would he do?"

"He'd kick Sonny's sorry ass back to Texas."

Sonny Campbell had a gift for making up excuses, and the

bigger the excuse it seemed the deeper blue his eyes would twinkle. We put calls in to Mitchell Mirage, pleading him to step in; after all, his high praise of Sonny got us here in the first place. But Mitchell's name was fitting—mirage, indeed—for he rarely called us back. When he did, his coughing fits rendered the conversation a total waste of time.

A month later the horror hit us: We had invested forty thousand dollars in Sonny Campbell. Half of that money came from our building allowance and the other half from Dad's blood, sweat, and tears. If we fired Sonny, how would we ever get our money back?

The following week we received a telegram. The last telegram that had come our way was from the World Bank expressing sympathies for Dad's sudden passing. So when Western Union came knocking again, we weren't expecting a Baci love note.

"Open it up, Francie."

"No, you . . ."

It was from the landlord and the gist of the telegram was: DUE TO FAILURE TO BEGIN CONSTRUCTION IN A TIMELY MANNER YOU ARE HEREBY IN DEFAULT OF YOUR LEASE STOP CONTACT BEN DICKINSON NO LATER THAN THE CLOSE OF BUSINESS TODAY OR THIS LEASE WILL BE TERMINATED STOP MARK PETERSON.

Francie, longing for peace of mind, a finished store, all things out of reach, moaned, "I need a Half-Moon Buttercream Dream."

We immediately had Ben on the phone. By now he knew that whenever we were on the line, we were both on the line. Two sisters in one.

"Calm down," he said, shy of comforting us. No "sweetheart," but definitely not as cutthroat as his colleagues. "We sent the telegram to document what's happening and to hopefully get your contractor on the ball. If not, well, you have no recourse but to threaten him with a lawsuit. If it comes to that, this telegram will help your case in court."

"A *lawsuit?*" Ginger cried. "You mean *sue* him?"

Francie's mantra coughed up. "I need a Half-Moon Buttercream Dream . . ."

"Look, I can recommend several small contractors to bid on your space; we have a Rolodex full of guys who would've gotten the job done in six weeks tops. I don't know where you found this one, but he sounds like a real loser."

Once Sonny Campbell got word of the telegram, he leaped into action. A minute later, it seemed, construction workers materialized with their tools and ladders and blueprints. Like worker ants in hard hats, they crawled in and out of the space and made plenty of noise that was music to our ears.

Compared to how good-looking and charismatic he had first seemed, to us, Sonny Campbell was now the ugliest man on earth. Still, no matter how much we despised him, it was in our best interest to stay with him and keep our payments up. By now it was late July, still plenty of time to open for Christmas. By mid-August, the foundation was poured and a frame for our shop was being nailed and bolted in place.

While our castle was being built, we busied ourselves trying to figure out the smaller stuff. From the Yellow Pages and industry catalogs, we ordered our nonchocolate needs: two modern cash registers and two state-of-the-art scales; candy trays in three distinct styles (not all chocolate shapes were created equal)—fluted silver, round glass, deep acrylic; boxes hot-stamped with our logo in every size imaginable—fancy silver ones for hand-picking gifts to give, white "baker" styles for hand-packing chocolates to go; and bags to match from a local company, Elman Labels. We whistled and sang, eating free samples like chocolate charms at Mom's kitchen

table. Of course we enjoyed them, but there was business at hand:
We had to decide which ones to include on our Chocolate Menu.
As if emceeing a bonbon beauty contest, Francie, with her air
mike, introduced our first contestant.

"Miss White with Bittersweet Truffle hails from San Francisco.
Quite curvy, she measures two by two."

Ginger grabbed the air mike. "Her intensely dark center is balanced by a creamy white shell, making her the ultimate truffle experience."

Francie took a taste and sized her up. "Definitely a finalist. Now
let's move on to Miss Cashew Cluster. While not as glam as some of
our other contestants, she's a nice fit in her fluted candy cup."

"Plain Jane," Ginger said, crossing it off our list. "No room for
Miss Congeniality here."

Mom grinned. "You two are crazy girl."

"And finally, we have Miss Cerise Kirsch," Francie continued.
"A knockout in red foil."

Ginger wolfed down three or four like they were m&m's. "Exactly what *is* kirsch?"

"Cherry liqueur."

"No wonder I'm buzzed," she cried, spitting out the last one.

Francie cast her vote. "She'll be a hit."

In mid-September, construction shut down. Assuring us that everything was on schedule, Sonny Campbell was still coming up with
excuses left and right.

"We're just waiting for materials . . .

"We've got a deadline on another project, but it'll be done on
Friday . . .

"We'll have the millwork installed by October . . ."

But October came and went and the only construction going on in the shop was the spiders building webs on our gorgeous Italian lights—appropriately macabre. By November, Sonny ran out of excuses and no longer took our calls, having turned the project over to an assistant whose breath smelled of ham. In too deep to turn around, we were left helpless and without direction, grateful for any little progress that was made.

By December, we had to accept that we would not be open for the holidays. The fact was sickening. We'd already purchased Christmas merchandise, now all dressed up with nowhere to go: chocolate Santas big and small, silver star-shaped boxes stuffed with star-shaped chocolates, a giant chocolate reindeer meant to be the centerpiece in our window now a sad tableau collecting dust at our headquarters. What would we do with all of it, how would we pay for it? The financial loss was incalculable to our young minds. All we understood was that it was a big blow.

Still, nothing could prepare us for the sight when the barricade came down in early January.

Our custom sign was nowhere to be seen. In blueprints, it was Broadway flash, designed of stainless steel with white letters that illuminated as dusk fell so that people walking or driving down Connecticut Avenue could see our name a block away. Where was it? Sonny Campbell had assured us it was finished last summer.

But the scene inside was even more horrifying.

The storefront was full of cracked glass windows, and the chrome shelving lining the walls was dented as crumpled tinfoil. Then Ginger made a fatal mistake: she looked down.

"What happened to the floor?!"

Instead of the watery black marble finish promised us, the floor was dull as a chalkboard, already scuffed white by the boots of construction workers.

Stepping inside, we were confronted by misaligned wall tiles. Groutless, some tiles had loosened from the wall and now lay on the ground, cracked and crumbled. Some things were just plain missing: the cabinet doors, a row of track lights, not to mention the three-compartment sink required for food service establishments. And what *was* there would have to be redone, replaced, *repaid* for, somehow. You could literally hear the place falling apart. A pep talk was in order.

Huddling: "We'll get through this . . ."

"Where there's a will, there's a way . . ."

When the bank confirmed that all of our checks to Campbell Construction were cashed, we were crushed. We knew we'd never see the money again. But we had no time for thoughts of revenge, at least not now, not yet. Our grand opening was two days away and we were already paying rent, so no matter what happened, we had to open for business.

From morning to midnight we worked cleaning our very dusty and dirty store. Mopping floors, wiping glass and counters, along with a few tears along the way. After two hours of this, Francie's heel got caught and broke off between two ungrouted tiles.

"What a nightmare," she hissed like she could strangle the air.

Ginger broke up laughing. "Next time, leave your stilettos at home."

Hobbling around with her bucket, Francie broke up, too.

We unpacked cases and stocked merchandise, taking in chocolate the whole time. Soon our moods lifted. Just the sight of it, the whiff of it, was enough to soothe the effect of the wreckage around us. And there, in our bombed-out shop, we realized that we had all the magic dust we'd need—each other and a shop full of chocolate.

Long after the streetlamps lit up and the city cleared out, we worked, until finally a hollow feeling came over us.

"Time to go home, Ginge."

The following morning, we perked up for the day ahead. We stacked trays in our glass cases high with rustic-looking Belgian truffles as well as our fragile crème fraîche pralines. We placed eye-catching gift-wrapped boxes in the windows to lure passersby. We gave our shop every ounce of chocolate love we had in us.

"It's beautiful," we kept murmuring, as if we couldn't quite believe it ourselves.

In spite of our setbacks, Chocolate Chocolate was already starting to shape up. Who knew, maybe we *could* sell a thousand dollars' worth of chocolates. Or was our wishful thinking just a Half-Moon Buttercream Dream?

Chapter 5

Manon Blanc

*A vanilla crème fraîche bonbon
laced with crème de cacao*

So here we were on opening day, two shivering sisters smiling at anyone who looked in our windows. Not that anyone actually *was* looking in. True, we didn't know a soul in the city and, true, we had no sign . . . But it was lunch hour, for God's sake. Where were all the "Chocolate Chocolate" chanters when we needed them?

We window-watched the world go by from our silent post. Cabs and couriers. Students with backpacks and professionals with briefcases. Everyone was in a hurry, even the old Ukrainian man with the cane. Well-heeled business types streamed through our building lobby toward the two high-profile restaurants on the terrace level. But did anyone spare a glance for our storefront? No.

What ever made us think we'd make it in this city?

It stung, a little. In 1984, few Asians populated the D.C. streets, and if we thought too hard about it, we'd become self-conscious and prickly.

"Let's put out samples," Ginger suggested.

Poof! A dozen Manon Blancs lay like pearls from an oyster on a tray on the counter. A trace of crème de cacao in the arctic air made them seem slightly illegal at this hour.

"Samples, anyone?"

We held our breath. The minutes ticked by. Five, ten, fifteen . . . The hush was eerily loud. You could have heard a dollar bill drop, if there were any dollars in sight. We fretted through the next hour, rearranging displays while our samples froze into snowballs.

With three walls of glass, our cube of a shop was illusively airy, divided into three areas: out front, behind the counter, and the back room. The main window was lined with shelves designed to draw people off the street with inviting displays: chocolate roses in chocolate vases; chocolate figurines of cats and frogs and pandas; chocolate monuments like Capitol Domes and Lincolns and White Houses. It was a theater of chocolate.

If windows could talk, ours would say: *Step inside and stay awhile. Warm up, smell the chocolate. Listen to the good music they've got playing. You may not know a soul on the street, but once you're inside, you've got someone to talk to. Welcome to Chocolate Chocolate.*

Out front was relatively roomy, where people could walk in off the street only to be engulfed in chocolate. First, they would be surrounded by the knockout, dizzying smell and, once recovered, encounter three candy cases brimming with bonbons. Across the countertop sat a small stack of Chocolate Menus and a long row of wooden racks of candy bars from Plain Milk to Bittersweet Framboise.

Behind the counter was perfectly cozy for two, and from here, we imagined, we would bring the Chocolate Chocolate experience to life: helping customers, packing boxes, ringing up sales, and creating beautiful clutter. The back room was a mere sliver of space, jam-packed with sweets and supplies under flickering fluorescent lights.

No matter where you were in the shop, you were always in the presence of chocolate. So what was wrong with Washington?

Francie was plopped down on a beat-up metal stool left behind by workers when a petite figure wobbled through the door. Was it—

"Stella!" we exclaimed.

"Hi, girls," she greeted us, windblown and weighed down by her red shoe bag and a weathered yellow tote. "How's the grand opening going?"

"Just grand," Ginger said sarcastically. "What's in the tote?"

Stella dropped it like a bag of trash. "Half-Moon Buttercream Dreams. They're all yours."

Francie swooned. "They're all *mine*."

"Stella, what's going on?" Ginger asked. Having another warm body in the shop was great, but a person doesn't drag free chocolate across state lines—from Maryland into D.C.—without good reason.

"What's going on is that I lost my job with Babe's last week when they decided to halt distribution on the East Coast. These Half-Moons were samples, and Babe's not getting them back, not over my dead body. I'm officially unemployed," she announced, making her way behind the counter like she lived there. "Look, kiddo"—she jabbed Francie—"I brought you enough Half-Moon Buttercreams to keep you smiling for life, the least you can do is offer me the stool." Once seated, she kicked off her black pumps and traded them for a pair of blue Keds. Primping her hair, she surveyed the shop. "Nice, girls, very nice."

So our favorite salesperson was out of work. We had a thought:

The rep for our local chocolate maker, Naron Candy Company, had retired not long after we placed our opening order.

"Why not give them a call?" Francie suggested.

Already Ginger was flipping through the Rolodex, for there was a lot to love about Naron, including their story.

When the owners, Mr. and Mrs. Naron, invited us for a tour of their facility the previous summer, old Baltimore came alive for us. Mr. Naron was bright eyed and nimble, Mrs. Naron, raspy voiced and hunched; he handled the chocolate making, she handled the books. Always together, they were high school sweethearts, married forty years. Legend had it that when Mr. Naron got out of the army after World War II, his father set him and his new bride up in business making chocolate. Not any old chocolate but homemade chocolates from family recipes, to be peddled on the streets of Baltimore.

"Girls, we still make our candies the way we did in the old days," Mr. Naron reminisced, showing us into a cooled-down room where a stout hair-netted lady was packing a box with chocolate-covered cherries. "We never cheat on ingredients."

"Never," punctuated Mrs. Naron as she passed by the doorway.

"High-grade cocoa beans," he continued, "never mock chocolate. Only pure vanilla, never extract. Only sugar, never corn syrup."

We could just picture the two, circa 1944, in a tiny commercial kitchen, reading recipes from old scraps of paper, mixing, heating, and cooling chocolate batter, forming chocolate balls by hand until every square inch of counter space was covered with trays of glistening bonbons. Then they would carefully stack the trays onto a little pushcart and take to the streets of Baltimore where Mr. Naron would handle the goods and Mrs. Naron would handle the cash in the hopes of making a life together.

However we romanticized the couple, their enterprise had

worked. In the years between, they had purchased a bigger commercial kitchen, but their philosophy of keeping things homemade and high quality was never lost.

The finery of European chocolate was in a league all its own, but we harbored a special love for American selections, too. Like chocolate marshmallows from a pushcart, the boxed candy of our youth would forever remain sweet.

Stella got off the stool and picked up the phone. "Ever since I was fourteen and working in my father's little shoe shop near Pittsburgh, I've been dreaming of the day I can retire and see the world, but that day isn't today. What's their number, Ginger?"

After lunch, Stella gone, a few bundled-up customers trickled in.

"Hi, how can we help you?"

Our breath made clouds in the cold shop air, and a woman wrapped in fluffy white fur cooed sympathetically.

"You girls look cold."

"The heat isn't working," Ginger explained.

"And the glass panes aren't tempered," Francie added. "One gust of wind, and there go the windows."

"Poor things." She took a closer look at us. "Sisters, right?"

"Right."

She reached for a sample. "And I bet you two have always stuck together."

"Always."

The woman in white fur grew sentimental. "I wish my sister lived close by."

Meanwhile, the sample tray was seducing her colleagues one by one. We watched them go weak in the knees over our Manon Blancs.

"I'd go to jail for this . . ."

"People, I'm having a religious experience here . . ."

"More like orgasmic . . ."

The whole shop had grown hearth warm. Here we had people eating, chatting, swooning.

A guy with slicked-back hair came up to the case. "So, is this your first day of business?" To our double nod: "So, how's it going?"

"Kind of quiet," Ginger admitted.

"Washingtonians are workaholics, glued to their desks." He shrugged. "I mean we're only here because there's a fire drill in our building." His nose twitched, as if bitten by crème de cacao essence. "You know what you girls need? An official grand opening party with free chocolate. *And* champagne! Who could resist? Invite the who's who in Washington. Every law firm and lobbyist. Send press releases to the *Dossier,* the *Post, Washingtonian.* That'll get the word out."

Now why didn't we think of that?

Within minutes we had picked a date for our official grand opening party: January 23, 1984.

Ginger rode the escalator down to the lower lobby level of our building, where Copy King ran big print jobs all day long. The manager, Ned, was an easygoing guy who was happy to make an announcement poster for us, as well as invitations. Plus, he happened to have a list of all the firms within a five-block radius. He'd let us borrow the golden list—as long as he could come to the party.

On the big night, the shop was sparkling with champagne flutes and a buffet of chocolates arranged on doily-covered silver platters. Our vendors had donated enough samples to titillate everyone in Washington. Miracle of miracles, the heat was finally working and we could slink out of our coats and show off our new outfits. Francie's hair was poofed even more than usual, and Ginger's eyelashes and bangs were curled. You never knew whom you might meet, especially if you believed in Bacis. Romance was in the air, as was music. During the day we were fickle with the radio dial, switching from top forty to golden oldies to progressive rock. But smooth jazz was bringing down the house tonight.

Ginger, the designated bartender, set out three rows of champagne flutes. "Should I pour the champagne now?"

"Not yet," Francie replied, wiping away a stubborn smudge on the candy case. "We don't want the bubbles bursting before the guests arrive."

"I wonder how many people will show up."

"Well, we sent out hundreds of invitations. But pour conservatively—we only bought one case of Freixenet."

We both looked out, expectant.

A half hour later, the shop was still empty.

"We said six o'clock, right?" Ginger was murmuring.

Francie looked at her watch. Six thirty. "Pour me a glass."

"Pour me one, too," ordered a voice out of nowhere.

It was Stella, coming through the lobby door. Her hair was blonder tonight and her lips were cherry red. "Congratulate me. I'm your official Naron Candy rep!"

Maybe now the night would get rocking. After a round of glass clinking, Stella looked around and huffed, "Where the hell is everyone?"

"Fashionably late." Ginger could only hope.

"I can't believe the local press didn't show."

"Maybe their invitations got lost in the mail," Francie suggested, growing glum. Not even manager Ned or the guy who suggested the party were coming.

"Ginger, darling"—Stella held up her empty champagne flute—"another round."

More time passed with us waiting for the doors to open. Six forty . . . six fifty . . . When the door finally opened, all three of us practically ganged up on our first guest of the evening, a small woman whose Eskimo parka disguised her from view.

Stella leaned over, trying to make out the face inside. She called as if through a foghorn, "My, you look very warm and fuzzy in there."

The woman shook off her hood to reveal a frosted brunette with big, expressive eyes. She was Francie's friend Carol. "I was."

After introducing her old friend to her new friend, Francie said, "Carol and I were college roomies, Stella."

"Oh, really? Then come behind the counter and get toasted with the family."

Carol's parka was off. "I'm coming."

Despite company and her buzz, Francie was still worried. When a few faces showed up, she brightened while Ginger began pouring the champagne, generously, for it was looking like we'd bought eleven bottles too many.

"Here for the party?" Ginger inquired.

"Uh, sure," one of them said.

Relieved, Francie pointed out our trays of chocolates galore. Even if they did just wander off the street, she was glad to see people in the store. Bodies. "Champagne and chocolate for everyone!"

Stella urged us to step out front and mingle. "Carol and I will preside behind the counter. Go on, go on."

Out front we balanced silver platters and began describing our chocolates in sumptuous detail. Ginger pointed out a white piece, as big as it was puffy, decorated with a swirl of dark chocolate.

"This one's called a White Mousse. It's light as air. You have to handle it with a delicate touch or it'll smoosh."

"What does it taste like?" they wanted to know.

"Like the richest wedding cake on earth," Francie described, washing one down with a little bubbly—nice finish.

Soon a few more faces joined our gathering until we had a body count of six, not including us. Only one, who brought a friend, was holding an invitation. The friend, dashing with dark wavy hair, exchanged a look with Ginger. A single look.

"So," Ginger dared to ask him, "where's *your* invitation?"

His boyish shrug made her feel faint. "What can I say?" He smiled. "It must've gotten lost in the mail. Maybe next time you can hand-deliver it to me." As if afraid he'd been too flirtatious too soon, he added, "By the way, my name is Rafael. I'm a junior attorney with a law firm on Sixteenth Street. And who are you, if I may ask?"

"I'm Ginger."

"Ginger in a candy store? I love it!"

As if no one else existed—indeed, his friend had already left—the two shared a laugh.

With a tray of chocolates in one hand and a tray of bubbly flutes in the other, Ginger was losing her balance in that delicious way every girl should feel at least once. "Chocolate or champagne?" she offered him.

He glanced at his watch. "No champagne tonight. I have a meeting down the street in ten minutes. But I'll take a chocolate." He reached for a Baci kiss, which he unwrapped and devoured with expertise.

"Did you know there's a little love note inside, Rafael?"

"Oh, I've had many a Baci in my time." He smiled, reading his fortune, then promptly crumpling it back into the foil and tucking it in his pocket.

"What did it say?" Ginger wanted to know. Desperately.

"It's a secret."

"A secret?"

"I'll tell you what it said another time." He glanced at his watch again. "I really have to go. It was great meeting you, Ginger-in-a-candy-store."

With that, Rafael was gone. And once he was gone, it was as if he was never here. The grand opening, duller than ever, never had a full house—the minute two people came in, two roamed out. No more cute guys. Almost everyone was getting sloshed.

"This party's flat," Francie said drunkenly into her sister's ear, "just like the champagne. By the way, who was the guy?" After Ginger filled her in, she predicted, "He'll return tomorrow with a dozen roses. In the meantime, let's make the most of this intimate soiree." Then Francie declared, "More champagne for everyone!"

Her shout seemed to spark an incident, for just then a chrome shelf in the storefront window collapsed to the floor.

BANG!

Everyone screamed, and Stella actually ran for cover, managing to hold on to her champagne flute.

"Oh, my God!"

"Was that an earthquake?"

Only Ginger was soberly assessing the situation. "Thank you, Sonny Campbell," she muttered.

The shelf had taken down a large basket twinkling with small silver boxes, each one hand-decorated with a satin ribbon and rose. Mom had a way of making everything look pretty, and she had worked so hard on those decorations. Every day she would call and ask, "Anyone buy today?"

Good thing Mom wanted to stay home tonight with Goldie and wasn't here to see her boxes all over the floor in a great big mess. It was hard to say, however, which sight was more sorrowful: Goldie, still waiting on the staircase for Dad to come home, her furry face turning white with age, or our shop—our dream—falling to pieces.

The next day looked more promising.

"Just as I predicted," Francie whistled when she spotted Rafael headed our way. He was carrying a single rose.

Ginger, shell-shocked: "You said a dozen roses."

"A single one is better."

"How so?"

"It means more."

"But how do you know it's for me?"

"It's got your name written all over it, Ginger-in-a-candy-store." Big Sis knew all the details.

After work, Rafael picked Ginger up at the shop, as she'd agreed without hesitation to go out for a drink with him. She didn't drink, actually, not after that one time in her teens when she'd gotten sick from unknowingly sipping grain punch like it was Kool-Aid, but perhaps she'd take a chance tonight.

"We'll look for the perfect bar and stop," he was saying. "Sound good, Ginger?"

"Sounds perfect."

In the starry dark, the two set out walking north on Connecticut Avenue and kept walking. It was cold, but they didn't feel a thing, only each other's presence. The conversation came easily and it seemed as though they could exchange their life stories in an hour or two or three. They walked all over the city, up to Dupont Circle and over to the West End, over to Georgetown to Foggy Bottom and back, walking and talking like nothing else mattered except this time together. Unfortunately, their time was running out: Rafael's law firm was transferring him to their Rome office. He spoke Italian and knew many of their clients.

"Rome?" Ginger nearly died. "When?"

He sighed. "Tomorrow."

"I don't believe this . . ."

"I was excited about starting my new life until I met you. Why didn't we meet earlier? Why didn't your shop open last year?"

Of course, our shop was *supposed* to open the year before, but Ginger spared him that story. Not when their time was clocked. Suddenly the two were standing in front of our shop.

"Hey," he realized sadly, "we never got our drink."

"We didn't need to," she said.

Almost awkwardly, Rafael thrust his business card in her hands, then squeezed them shut. "I took the liberty of writing down my Rome address for you on the back. Please write me. Who knows, I might be back someday, Ginger-in-a-candy-store."

Rafael embraced her, and they stood still for a long time, until their embrace melted into a long warm kiss, neither letting go as if they both sensed it would have to sustain them for a long time. Afterward, Ginger wanted to ask him what the Baci love note said. But somehow it felt too late.

A single rose.

A single walk.

A single kiss.

The week ended on a quiet note. As much as Ginger wanted to, she doubted she would write Rafael. He was gone and she couldn't wish him back. Whatever message was in his Baci love note, it did not include her.

Ginger's disappointed heart aside, we couldn't seem to pull in enough customers, no matter how many free samples we offered. On the rare occasion someone walked in empty-handed and walked out balancing bags, we fooled ourselves into believing all our troubles were over. But when the next hour was dead, our optimism withered. For so long, our mythical castle, Chocolate Chocolate, had been a sugar-spun fantasy, and going bankrupt was something that happened in Monopoly. However, these days we were facing a harsh reality—if we didn't start selling chocolate soon, we were going to lose our business.

Thank God there was always tomorrow.

On Tuesday, the last morning of the month, with ten minutes to spare before opening, we walked over to Vie de France to grab a single cup of black coffee, extra Styrofoam cup, to go, please— pinching pennies meant sharing coffee. Then we trudged to our shop as our spirits were already sinking. Yet once we unlocked the doors and turned on the lights, the smell of chocolate revived us.

"There aren't words . . ."

". . . in the English language . . ."

Chocolate, bottled up all night, was absolute heaven. The subtler notes of vanilla, caramel, and liqueur sang their siren songs. Francie set our coffee cup on a green transformer in the back room to keep it warm.

"Time to work," she declared.

Surrounded by chocolate, nothing was a chore. We piled chocolates high on trays, wrapped boxes, dusted, and worked on orders.

"Time for coffee," Ginger announced.

With chocolate, of course! That day, like so many, we ended up eating more than we sold. Chocolate was in our blood; it sustained us. And its ritualized comfort was something we'd learned about early on. After all, no one knew more about its special powers than Mom.

～

As a girl in Sinuiju, a northern Korean city on the Yalu River, Mom's life had been privileged. She was spoiled by her five much older brothers, who showered her with gifts—shoes from London, a gold watch from Shanghai. The political struggles of her country seemed far removed from her world. Who could worry when there were plump sweet bean cakes to enjoy? Jelly candies from Tokyo? And her favorites: chocolates from Manchuria?

But this way of life ended when the Japanese forced all Koreans into the war effort of World War II. One day she was playing piano; the next day, sewing buttons on soldiers' uniforms. Food supplies dried up; schoolmates disappeared, along with her Fifth Brother, who was drafted into the war to fight for the Japanese against his will. Then, unspeakable tragedy: Her Second Brother and his family, living in Peking, were massacred by Mao Tse-tung followers.

Once the Korean War broke out, Russians began invading the north, driving millions of Koreans south to escape Communist control. Mom's family decided it was safer to stagger their escapes and eventually reunite in Seoul. As it was, her mother couldn't leave yet, not until her Fifth Son made his way home from the war. He was coming home, she was sure of that.

Once her father and three brothers had made it to the south, the day came for Mom to make her escape. She was only sixteen, so her parents had hired a guide to take her there, a guide who knew the safest route. *No, no, no*, she kept saying, kept begging, *I don't want to go*—but she had no say. When she hugged her mother good-bye, she had no idea how the memory of that night would haunt her.

Soon she found herself alone, a refugee roaming the streets of Seoul. How could this possibly happen? She shook her head, trying to remember her old life, but the bombs were too loud, and she could barely hear her own voice cry for her mother.

"*Oma . . .*"

Seoul teemed with refugees like her trying to reunite with their families. Desperation high, people crowded in coffee shops and combed through newspapers, hoping to catch a loved one's notice. At schools and churches, notes were posted on bulletin boards. It was on one such bulletin board at Ewha University that fortune smiled on Mom; she recognized the handwriting of her father who, along with three of her brothers, was looking for her.

Reunited, the cobbled-together family found sleeping quarters in a church. At night they sang songs and wept for the wife and mother who stayed behind, waiting for her youngest son to return from war.

Even with money in her pocket and a floor to sleep on, Mom was no better off than a beggar: Rice was rationed; the markets were bare. One day she passed a small market, its shelves nearly empty except for . . . Was she hallucinating from hunger? Before her was a tantalizing mirage, a barrel filled with the biggest chocolate bars she had ever seen. Brown wrappers, English lettering. Gasping, she asked the shopkeeper, "Where did you get these?"

"The Communists invaded the American PX and sold them to me," he said in a whisper.

Black-market chocolate. What could possibly be more delicious? Mom emptied her pockets without a second thought.

That night, as American B-52s dropped bombs over Seoul, the rooming house next door going up in the smoke, shrapnel shattering the church window over her head, Mom hid under a thick burlap blanket with her Hershey bars. She comforted herself with a vow: "If I must die, I will die with chocolate on my lips!"

During our childhoods, Mom always wore a brave face. Sometimes we would hear her quietly weeping behind walls, or see her face contorting with emotion while stirring fiery *chigae* stew, but we knew better than to ask questions—those were lines you didn't cross. As kids, we had no idea that the sudden yank from her idyllic childhood had set a reclusive tone for the rest of her life, or that she worried every day over the fate of her mother, or that her Third Brother, her most beloved and most doting, was killed the night she nibbled on an American chocolate bar to the echoing sounds of bombs close by.

We understood only that she stashed family-sized Hershey bars in our big egg-yolk-colored fridge, deep inside, hidden behind the milk and orange juice. Unlike the milk and orange juice, the chocolate bars in the brown wrappers were forbidden to us—they were hers and hers alone. She never came out and said so; she didn't have to. They were out of sight, as was she when she was nibbling, or so she thought. But we saw her, sometimes. There, standing in the streaming kitchen sunlight, eating her chocolate and staring out the window as if she could see through trees. Her breathing slow, her eyes so still, the chocolate lingering on her lips . . . Oblivious to the phone ringing or the teakettle whistling, she seemed to have drifted off into a world completely foreign to us.

While we were well aware of the power of chocolate, it seemed the rest of the world wasn't. As January came to a close, dusk swept through a sweetshop bereft of laughter, light, and customers. It was heartbreaking not to see a growing clientele. The phone rang— Mom, as usual. She always called after hours, as if a part of her was still hiding.

"How is business today?"

Ginger couldn't hide the glum report. "Not so hot, Mom."

After she hung up, we just sat there in the soundless dark. Every flaw Sonny Campbell left behind stood out like neon lighting. Our dream shop had morphed into an ugly, scratched, not-worth-fixing neon nightmare.

"Maybe," Francie said as if she'd just cracked some secret code, "we're missing something here."

"Like what?"

"Like our very own trademark bonbon."

"Oh, no," Ginger wailed, "not this again."

"Why so resistant? I don't get it."

"Are you insane? We're already over our heads with the shop. Besides, I like making things for you and Mom, not the whole world. And making chocolate isn't anything like baking brownies."

"But you could whip up anything you wanted, Ginge. I know it, I can feel it."

"Drop it," Ginger begged her.

And so Big Sis did. For now.

Chapter 6

Chocolate Heart, Foiled

Rich milk chocolate love

February 1984. A rumor was going around that this was the month of love, but frankly, you could've fooled us. Without boyfriends—or enough business—to keep us busy, love was the last thing we felt like celebrating. By now we'd traded in Baci love notes for the deep red foil of milk chocolate hearts—not a bad substitute for love. The act of slowly peeling off the foil—crumple, *ping!*—then popping a smooth, heart-sculpted chocolate in your mouth was a truly sensual experience; your eyes would close and you could almost hear Etta James singing "At Last." So when a bulldog of a guy stormed into the shop on a late Wednesday afternoon, it was all we could do to lift our eyelids and steady ourselves. That's what happens when you're drunk on chocolate.

Short and stocky, the man began making all kinds of demands as soon as he'd gotten the door open: "Look, I got a plane to catch and I'm in a hurry!" He marched right over and continued in a heavy Boston accent, "Where's the biggest Valentine's box ya got?"

Ginger struggled to present a keepsake box too heavy to hold with one hand as the man shifted impatiently. Hard to believe there was a world where both Bulldog and Rafael breathed the same air. She forced a smile. "How about this?"

Originally designed as a sewing basket, Mom, with the help of her trusty glue gun, had topped the box's lid with a foam pillow, then covered it with red satin and white lace. Carefully applied tiny pearls and dried flowers were the crowning glory—each box took two hours of painstaking work. In Vanna White fashion, Francie flipped up its lid to reveal dozens of red-foiled chocolate hearts. But her Dentyne smile was suddenly upstaged by an explosive noise. The two of us exchanged a look of utter shock, and Bulldog swung around.

"Sheesh! What the hell was that?" he said.

Ginger moaned. "Just our store going to pieces."

A wall tile near the front door had come unglued and crashed to the floor. Had Bulldog been in its path, he'd probably be history. Since he wasn't, and since he couldn't care less about our shop, his attention turned back to the Valentine keepsake box Francie was still holding.

"No, no, I want something bigger and heart shaped," Bulldog barked, growing more disgruntled.

Desperate to keep our store afloat, we were at the mercy of anyone who walked in with a wallet. Luckily, a large, plush, frilly velvet heart caught his eye.

"Like that!"

With a hefty price tag of ninety-five dollars, that purchase would double our receipts for the day.

"Sure," Ginger said, "that costs—"

"I don't care how much it costs," he said, dropping bills on the counter. "I need it delivered two blocks away by six thirty—can you do that?"

For ninety-five dollars?

"Sure!"

"Good," he said, now filling out an enclosure card, then scribbling an address on the front of the envelope.

"We need a suite number, too," Ginger informed him. In a land of office buildings, a suite number was a must.

"No suite number," he said. "It's going to Silhouettes."

From our days of scoping out the town looking for locations, we knew that Silhouettes was sandwiched in between several run-down bars and cafés whose tarnished awnings defined M Street between 18th and 19th. We always skipped that side of the street. But for this sale, we'd hand-deliver his Valentine to Silhouettes at no extra charge.

"It's for Dee Dee," he said, waving away his receipt, "and don't be late."

At six o'clock we closed up shop and headed toward Silhouettes in a monster wind-whipping cold. Our long hair wrapped around our faces.

"Ugh, Ginge, I hate the cold!"

"Yeah, but you gotta love the cold, hard cash."

Once we crossed the street to Silhouettes and actually stood on this stretch of sidewalk, X-rated vibes and sewer fumes engulfed us. This was no place for puppy love. Two husky bouncers who stood by the door were a dead giveaway.

Our warbled hellos brought both bouncers to life in a kinky-winky kind of way. They were sizing us up: two sisters, windblown hair.

"Ladies," the first bouncer greeted us, "you here to apply for the job?"

"No."

"Aw, c'mon! Ya look like exotic dancers."

"Uh . . ."

"Ya never danced in a gentlemen's club?" the second bouncer chimed in. "Try it, you'll like it!"

"We're not here to be dancers," Francie expressed in her most professional tone. "We're here to deliver—"

"The girls here pull in three hundred on a slow night," Bouncer number one interrupted. "On that, you could rent in the Watergate and drink Dom Perignon in your bubble bath. Think about it—the two of you'd make a good act."

We already did, at our own establishment where the street signs didn't flash GENTLEMEN ONLY over the sidewalk.

"A customer wanted us to deliver this to someone named Dee Dee," Ginger said, handing him the tote. "Can you please give this to her?"

"Depends. What's inside?"

"Chocolate."

"Okay, sure, if I can have a piece." Wink, wink.

We humored them with forced smiles, worried that otherwise they might gobble up the contents and toss the empty heart in the alley. As we turned to leave, bouncer number two called after us.

"Think about it, ladies! Bill yourselves as 'Double Trouble' and you'll pull in a grand a night, easy!"

On the way back to our shop, Ginger huffed, "I can't believe they wanted us to be strippers."

But for a grand a night, it was actually tempting.

If customers weren't breaking down our doors, at least the confection industry was excited that our doors were open. Magazines flooded our mailbox, and most days, with nothing to do but dust shelves, we glanced through them all, picking up a few things we hadn't learned in our SBA course. For example, January was the slowest month for sweetshops; either people were broke from Christmas, had leftover stocking treats, or were on New Year's resolution diets. We'd actually survived that month, so maybe the worst was over.

And maybe things were starting to pick up just a little. One Friday evening at precisely six o'clock, just as Francie was jingling her keys to lock up, a young blond woman in a red coat stopped in.

"Are you still open?"

In no position to turn anyone away, we'd stay open to midnight for a sale. Francie dropped her keys back in her purse. "Of course we're open."

"I'll just be a minute," she promised.

"Oh, take your time," Ginger said, obliging her from behind the counter. It wasn't as if we had anywhere to go. Besides, Ginger thought maybe she recognized her from Fridays past, a petite thing in high heels straining to see the merchandise on top of our cases. "And let me know if I can answer any questions."

"Actually, yes. I'm looking for those tiny boxes that are usually in a basket right here on the counter." The woman tilted her head up with the rise of her voice, as if no other box would do. "Did you sell out of them today?"

Not exactly. Earlier that day, our heat went on the blink, and a maintenance engineer in the building who took pity on our situation placed a temporary heater up on a ledge near the ceiling. The blasts of warm air, directed right at us, were heavenly—that is, until we realized that all of our merchandise on top of our candy cases had melted, including the ring-sized boxes that housed one solitary bonbon.

"If you give me just a minute," Ginger offered, "I'd be happy to make one up for you."

Beaming, the customer clasped her hands. "That's so nice of you!"

When she left, Francie remarked, "She's a sweetheart. We've seen her before, right?"

Ginger nodded. "I believe she comes in every Friday."

A repeat customer? We took it as a good sign.

Another small step in the right direction: We found a new contractor, Gary Goldman, to clean up and fix Sonny Campbell's mess, or at least the necessities like having permanent glass panes installed and the two illuminated custom signs promised us so long ago. It was costly, but we had no choice. Examining our chalky floors, he shook his very bald head with disgust.

"It's guys like him who ruin it for the rest of us. Do you two know what's wrong with these floors?"

"Everything," we replied.

"Campbell substituted wall marble to go on the floor. Believe me, when it was installed, it was shinier than this head of mine. But wall marble's meant to stay on walls, not be subjected to workers and scaffolds leaving their mark—sorry to say, permanently."

"I take it wall marble is cheaper," Francie deduced.

"Half the price," Gary said. "That way he had twice as much to gamble away at Atlantic City."

We croaked.

"Sorry, I heard it through the grapevine. Electricians can be such gossips," he joked, trying to lighten up the situation. "Sounds like the guy was over his head and had a meltdown."

We didn't give a damn; the blue-eyed bastard was going to pay for this.

"Well, can we get new floors?" Ginger wanted to know.

Gary explained that new floors were exorbitantly expensive and weren't in the budget. We were just going to have to live with what we had, along with smaller blemishes like crooked grout lines and sloppy millwork with nicks everywhere. Taking pity on our fallen faces, Gary ordered a small box of Peanut Butteries for his wife. "On second thought, make that a big box."

The good news? Gary had two temporary signs made in a matter of hours, one that hung above our street door and one above our lobby door. With the flick of a switch, the signage attracted a few more customers every day. Later that week he poked his head in with a thumbs-up. "Just wanted to tell you two we got a new estimate for your glass, and it looks like the cost of your job's going to be less than we thought."

Thumbs-up.

The next Friday, at the stroke of six, the shop was empty. Hushed.

"Where's 'Our Girl Friday'?" Ginger wondered.

"I bet she's coming."

Sure enough, Our Girl Friday dashed in. Her face was flushed from running in the cold and her voice was breathless. "I'm so glad you're still open!"

"We were waiting for you," Ginger said. "One box to go, right?"

"Right." She laughed, digging for her wallet. "I'm on my way to Union Station to catch a train to Philly—my boyfriend lives there. If I didn't show up with his box, he'd be crushed. I know it's silly, isn't it? But it's already a tradition every Friday night. Do you know what I mean?"

Of course we did. We spoke the language of chocolate.

"See you next Friday," she said, casting a loving gaze at her box before dropping it in her handbag. Then Our Girl Friday disappeared into the night.

Making progress in fixing up the store and having a regular customer (even if only one) made the dark days of February easier to get through. On the second Monday of the month, Ginger picked Francie up for work. Theoretically, Francie could've walked to work, but not in those high heels.

In typical fashion, we sang our way into town, accompanied by "Girls Just Want to Have Fun." Just as we parked in the building's underground garage, Francie's contact lens popped out and, like so many before it, was lost forever.

"Think I have time to go to Atlantic Optical?" Francie wondered on the elevator ride up. As a girl, she was always breaking or losing her eyeglasses; now it was her contacts. Atlantic Optical kept a spare pair in stock for her at all times.

"Go, go," Ginger urged her.

Tomorrow was Valentine's Day. Fingers crossed, we had upped our inventory to include some Valentine's Day items. Not a ton, just enough to set a mood and remind the public that, for some lucky people, love was in the air and it was time to buy chocolate. Thanks to Sonny Campbell, Chocolate Chocolate was no natural beauty, but with a little satin, lace, and TLC she could still be quite the stunner. Now the shop was all dressed up with red tins chock-full of Swiss truffles, heart-shaped Belgian pralines wrapped in cellophane, and ruby-wrapped gifts to go. We hoped we'd get a little extra traffic, but weren't counting on it. Most likely, one person could man the shop.

But as we entered our store, we saw a crowd of anxious men in wool coats lined up outside both doors. Francie's other contact nearly popped out.

"What's going on, Ginge?"

"I guess it's the day before Valentine's Day!"

Francie's trip to Atlantic Optical would have to wait. We had customers—*plural*—to wait on.

The minute we unlocked our doors, the mob was grabbing anything and everything off the shelves—chocolate dust, if we had it. The biggest hits were the Swiss champagne truffles we had discovered at the Fancy Food Show, slipped into silver boxes of every size. But an hour in, when we sold out of all our prepacked gifts to go, tempers flared. For every impatient male flicking his gold American Express card and glancing at his watch, we were hand-packing a box that was taking too much *#/!* time.

"Miss, could you hurry it up?"

"Look, I've got a meeting in ten minutes!"

"Where's your hired help, for God's sake? Don't you know it's Valentine's Day?"

No kidding. Around noon, all hell broke loose. Chocolates, boxes, and scissors were flying. While the phone was ringing off the hook, men were jostling for our attention—and they weren't exactly whispering sweet nothings in our ears.

"Hey, I'm next!"

"Over here, damn it!"

Now that we'd seen half the men in town, a valid question was

in order: Were two young women like us ever going to find love in
this city?

Ginger grumbled between customers, "We may as well be hid-
eous old hags."

"Don't look in the mirror," Francie called over the noise of yelling customers while clamping down on the credit card machine.
"Your hair's turned white!"

The back room became a fire hazard, cluttered with so much
trash you couldn't step in there without tripping. At one point,
Francie kicked through the back door to take a five-second break
just to give her blurry eyes a rest from the utter insanity.

"I'd rather be dancing at Silhouettes!"

Focus. Breathe.

Yet every now and then, in the midst of this pre-Valentine's
frenzy, we managed to steal looks only we could read: *Is this really
happening? We're gonna be rich! Millionaires in months!*

We faced the next day with dread and elation. If Valentine's
Day was half as hectic as the day before, we'd need a team of ten to
help us out, but since we didn't have the money to hire staff, the
two of us would have to do. We got in early, before eight A.M., so
we could prepare for the day—restock the empty candy cases and
preassemble as many boxes as we could. No sooner did we turn on
the lights than men began pulling on the doors. We shook our
heads, *Sorry, no.* We needed this time to set up in peace. *Please go
away.* They wouldn't listen. The only person we let in was Stella,
who unexpectedly showed up with a dolly full of emergency Valentine heart-shaped boxes.

"I'd stay and help out, but my arches are aching. Knock 'em
dead, girls!"

At eight forty-five, Francie left the shop to run over to Atlantic

Optical to pick up a replacement contact. She couldn't face another day as a one-eyed ogress.

Upon her return, she was shocked to see the store open for business in the dark. Ginger was in hysterics, single-handedly trying to wait on every man in the shop. Why'd she open so early? And why weren't the lights turned on?

Ginger tied a giant red velvet bow around a box, madly stuttering, "When you left you forgot to lock the door behind you! Men just trampled in, and I couldn't get them to leave! They wouldn't listen to me!"

Men in line on Valentine's Day are not exactly at their most gracious, especially if they're late for appointments. They may be perfect gentlemen every other day of the year, but when they're shoving one another left and right and the phone won't stop ringing, they're downright scary. So when an unsuspecting female wandered into the shop to buy a candy bar, oblivious to this day of, ahem, *love*, a near riot broke out. Men started shouting, "Get in line, lady!"

The woman plopped her money on the counter and chuckled. "A little sympathy for a single woman, fellas."

After hours, doors locked, we flipped off the lights despite a small crowd of men outside both doors, knocking, begging, waving credit cards and big bills. We didn't have the energy to ring up one more sale. Collapsing onto the floor mats behind the counters, we waited for them to go away, then took in the quiet. Had there ever been a more beautiful hush?

"It's over."

"Amen to men."

～～～

The St. Valentine's Day massacre of 1984 left nothing behind besides crumbs on trays and dust on shelves—not a single foiled chocolate heart in the house.

We knew that when we were little white-haired ladies in side-by-side rockers, we'd still be talking about that day, the hordes of frantic men and the sassy lady who put them in their place. But right now we were too exhausted to talk. Two days of chaos had taken their toll. Only chocolate could restore us.

"We deserve a treat."

"What's left?"

From her handbag, Francie retrieved one of the small silver boxes Mom hand-decorated. Perhaps from the light of a streetlamp or passing headlights, the box gleamed in the dark. Inside were two champagne truffles from Altdorf, Switzerland. Powdered sugar made them twinkle slightly in the dim light.

"I saved this for us."

There was an irony about working like a dog during Valentine's when you didn't even have a Valentine. Not a card, not a kiss, nothing. For us, these gems were a godsend.

They blew the Bacis out of the water. Who needed a love note—or a man, for that matter—when you've got Swiss truffles?

"These are amazing, don't you think?"

A look, slow and puzzled, crossed Ginger's face. "Yeah . . . but . . . is there something in here besides champagne?"

"I don't think so."

Yet something tasted tingly. Laced. In a sense they tasted foiled—and not in the way of our milk chocolate hearts.

"My lips feel kind of numb . . ."

"So does my throat . . ."

It didn't last long. A drink of water later, we could feel our lips again. But what was causing the funny sensation?

The fear that we would be hit with complaints and returns—if not lawsuits—prompted us to agree to submit samples of the Swiss chocolates to the FDA. We weren't the manufacturer, so we told ourselves we weren't legally responsible, but what if the tainted truffles destroyed our reputation one month after opening our doors for business? Worse, what if the chocolate was laced with something dangerous?

Wednesday the sun rose and we wanted to stay in bed. We shuddered to think about what the day would bring: hundreds of men who purchased Swiss Altdorf truffles for Valentine's Day. Soon they'd be storming in, threatening to sue—after all, every other man in D.C. was a lawyer. Knowing our distress, Mom offered to leave her Yamagada cards behind and come in with us for moral support.

"No one yell at old lady," she assured us.

At fifty-four she was hardly old. True, she was the matriarch. Still, whenever she went out in public, her stately beauty put us to shame, and we couldn't help but recall our youth when neighborhood boys would make excuses to come over—*Hi, Mrs. Park!* Even now, all she needed was a dab of lipstick and she was out the door.

Sure enough, at ten A.M. sharp, the first male customer arrived at the scene of the crime. He was fortyish, in a million-dollar suit.

"Hi, ladies."

Like paper dolls, we clutched hands behind the candy case.

"Hellooo . . . ," we replied, our voices pitched higher than usual.

He sniffed around the shop, no doubt looking for evidence against us. We held our breath while Mom, in an uncharacteristic move, took the lead.

"How I can help you today?"

"I'm looking for those Swiss truffles you sell. I bought a box of them for Valentine's Day yesterday."

While Mom bravely soldiered onward, we were still clutching hands beneath the counter. "Oh, your wife like them?"

"No . . ."

We stopped breathing.

"She *loved* them"—he laughed heartily—"and sent me back for more."

All three of us exhaled.

"Oh, she have good taste," Mom said, so happy. "She is alcoholic?"

"Excuse me?"

"She means a *choco*holic," Ginger clarified, taking over the sale.

Similar scenes replayed that morning and afternoon with Mom at the helm. Enjoying this role, she celebrated by digging into a Chocolate-Dipped English Toffee—alas, it was too sticky for her and ended up in the trash. Fear not, Maple Creams were another favorite, their aroma deep enough to make you swoon. But today they intensified Mom's liberation while she chatted with customers like she'd been here, in the shop, her whole life.

"Uh-oh," Ginger croaked, "look at Mom!"

Free of her usual reserve, Mom was in fine butterfly form, flitting from customer to customer, many of whom were looking for belated Valentine's gifts. Our inventory was low, but she showed what was left, full of warm gestures and smiles, all the while not realizing something: There was a huge hole gaping out of her mouth.

"Mom," Francie said, trying to step into her sale.

Having way too much fun, Mom ignored her. "You find own customer," she said over her shoulder.

When the place cleared out, Francie, not knowing whether to laugh or cry, gently broke the news to her that her front tooth was missing. When Mom saw her reflection in the mirror above the cash register, she instinctively covered her mouth.

"Oh, no . . . ," she gasped.

"Mom," Francie asked, "do you think you might've swallowed it?"

Her hand dropped. "I don't know . . ."

"Wait a minute," Ginger said, digging through the trash. Soon she held up a piece of English Toffee, the one earlier tossed. Sometimes detective work paid off, for Mom's bridgework was stuck to it. "Voilà!"

Overcome with relief, Mom laughed. Toothless or not, she was coming out of her shell.

Men, we learned, return to their normal if not mild-mannered selves the day after Valentine's Day. Still, for the next week, each time one walked through the door, we braced ourselves for conflict. To our surprise, not one customer came back angry or alarmed over the funky Swiss truffles. In fact, everyone, along with their wives and girlfriends, was craving *more* of them.

But, question: Did anyone experience the lip-throat numbing effect we did?

Yes, and they *loved* it. Indeed, one customer likened the sensation to fugu sashimi, a Japanese delicacy where a minute amount of poison in blowfish causes a prickly numbness on a diner's tongue and lips. Too much can kill you, but apparently delectable danger turned some people on. The only complaint our customers had was when we decided to stop stocking the Swiss line until we got to the bottom of this mystery. Like addicts, they kept begging for more.

In time, the FDA analysis revealed that the mysterious ingredient responsible for the numbing effect was a new preservative that, when used too heavy-handedly, can cause a temporary numbing sensation. Fortunately, it wasn't dangerous or illegal, just weird. When we called the well-meaning Swiss father-son Emminger team, they admitted that, nervous about the shelf-life of their U.S.-bound truffles, they had added preservatives without telling us.

Love is all about trust and we couldn't help but feel deceived. So in the end, our love affair with Swiss Altdorf was—like so many love affairs—short-lived. Still, we had survived February and the Valentine's Day Massacre, and we were somewhat hopeful that business would continue to grow. As for love? Maybe, just maybe, a new affair was just around the corner.

Chapter 7

Milk Chocolate
Mousse Dream

*A chocolate sugarplum of
marbleized milk and white chocolate,
crowned with a walnut*

Before love, revenge. Sweet revenge. Finding the perfect lawyer, however, wasn't as easy as finding the perfect chocolate, so for the time being we sought refuge in Neuhaus, famed for whipping hazelnuts into chocolate. They churned out their *gianduja* in so many irresistible shapes and sizes you had to sink your teeth into all of them, over and over. An Escargot, a Horseshoe, a Pharaoh . . . Among our favorite was the dollar sign—one rich, nutty whiff and we were goners. Ah, if only dollar signs were a method of payment, then we'd have the means to hire a top-notch lawyer to sue that scum ball contractor Sonny Campbell. What a delicious thought.

Law firms in our building represented politicians and CEOs, not two penniless sisters. So in late February we met with a lawyer we found named Neil Schultz in nearby Georgetown. His ad in the Yellow Pages indicated that his specialties were construction and personal injury lawsuits, claiming, "I won't charge you an arm and a leg—even if you lost one." Maybe we could afford him.

"Call me Neil," he insisted while seating us at a gleaming glass-top conference table crowned with a crystal vase of exotic orchids. Despite his Italian-cut suit, there was something unkempt about him, like he missed his five o'clock shave.

"Perrier?" he offered us.

"No, thanks," Ginger said.

A young assistant zipped in, opened the floor-to-ceiling blinds to reveal a panoramic view of the Potomac at night, and zipped out.

"Beautiful, isn't it?" He smiled.

Growing wary, we had to remind ourselves that this was a free consultation and thanked him for meeting with us after hours.

"It's not after hours here," he said. "Now, tell me everything."

While we spilled our guts, Neil took notes, bearing ornate rings on half his fingers.

This meeting was doomed, but heck, we were here so we decided to stay long enough to hear his take on the Sonny Campbell matter.

"Ladies, this is going to be a tough case, a very tough case . . ."

Ka-ching.

"But there's no doubt in my mind that with a lot of hard work on my part, I can win it for you . . ."

Ka-ching.

"Naturally, I'll require a retainer fee . . ."

Ka-ching.

"...and my hourly fee is two hundred and fifty dollars—cab fare compared to your award."

Translation: You're paying for this breathtaking view, the flowers, my kids' tuition, *and* an arm and a leg.

We met with one, two, three more lawyers, but it was always the same story: money, money, and more money. One day a sympathetic customer mentioned a childhood friend who was now a lawyer. She described George Geibel as an off-the-wall guy who had more passion for his music than his career. Nevertheless, he had a winning record and a good heart. Something about him sounded promising to us, and in wishful moods, we gave him a call. Since George didn't have a real office, our initial consultation took place over the phone.

"Sometimes I sublet office space, but right now I'm working from home in Bethesda," he said.

"Great, because we can't even afford to pay you babysitting fees," Francie freely admitted.

"We're broke," Ginger cried. "*Broke.*"

Aside from memories, Valentine's Day didn't make us rich after all, and, darn, it came only once a year. In our hushed-again shop, our bank account dwindled to nothing, with bills mounting, creditors calling, and our construction nightmares—indeed, tearing checks from their perforation hurt like hell. Even Mom's surprise refund from the IRS—ten thousand dollars that she promptly donated to our cause—was gone in a matter of minutes.

Our accountant, Chuck, who had indicated that he'd make some calls, suggested we apply for a loan, which led to a series of stressful experiences. No bank in town would lend us a dime, not unless we offered up Mom's house as collateral. For a million reasons—the least of which being that she'd kill us—the very notion brought tears to our eyes. This was Dad's American dream, the sun yellow Colonial surrounded by gardens. His green thumb was famous—touch a bud, watch it bloom. In the warmer months, after a long day at the office, he could often be found watering his trellis of roses that glorified the side of the house, or tending to the wall of bamboo he planted deep in the backyard to muffle the noise of traffic. His yard was his Eden.

The spring after he died, a curious thing happened: Except for the bamboo, nothing grew back. No roses or rhododendrons or azaleas. And just as curious, we never questioned it. That the yard died with him seemed as natural as earth itself.

When Dad wasn't in his garden, we could find him in his garage-converted den, a room so cold we wondered how he got his work done. Peek in, and there he was in that maroon sweater vest, sitting next to a small coal-black heater working its heart out.

Dad, it's an ice box in there!

So? Come join me . . .

In the five years since his shocking death at age fifty-six, not a thing in there had been touched. Not a pen, not a paper clip . . .

Our loss was still life.

On the wall above Dad's desk hung a reminder of his boyhood poverty, a portrait of his family circa 1929, when he was six. The only photograph taken of him as a child showed a boy with a princely face, sadly malnourished, and wearing clothes more suited for a boy half his age. Growing up, we passed that portrait thousands of times, never once pausing to reflect on what it all meant. Dad preferred it that way. In a home that was his palace, he created a world safe and far removed from the image of a hungry child with hollow eyes.

No collateral, period.

Yet we were desperate. Too many days our cash register tallied less than a hundred dollars. "Double-digit-dead" days, we called them.

The next day, a guy parked his Harley out front and sauntered in. With exaggerated flourish he took off his motorcycle helmet and began playing air guitar. Ginger was busy describing the velvety high you got from a Grand Marnier chocolate cream to a first-time customer while Francie was tempting a tourist with whiffs from the sample tray. She was talking up Coeur de Chocolat, a brand-new imported line that overnight was taking the country by storm. Unlike the more traditional Neuhaus, these were touted as "nouvelle cuisine" chocolates. Using less sugar per batch, the chocolates were intense, yet so light and airy a fingerprint would dent them.

"That means you can eat twice as many," Francie kidded anyone who was listening.

Once the shop was empty, the guy was still there, rocking out like Van Halen. Francie wasn't sure whether to laugh or call security, but to be on the safe side, she poised her finger on the phone's red panic button. When pushed, a security guard would appear within sixty seconds. "Can I help you?"

"I'm George Geibel," he introduced himself. "You must be Francie."

Relief. "How'd you guess?"

"Your voices," he explained. "Ginger's still hoarse from all that yelling on the phone yesterday." His wink spurred Ginger on.

"Well, that Sonny Campbell has gotta hang by his . . ."

He teased her. "You're the baby in the family, right?"

"How'd you know?"

"The youngest is always the ballsiest."

George was now studying the shop, its damaged face behind all the charming chocolates and other pretty things. Okay, the major work like installing permanent glass was done, thank you, but eyesores still disgraced every corner from scratched cases to unfinished cabinetry, from scarred chrome to ruined floors. Those, we had to live with.

"Don't worry, guys," George concluded.

Francie questioned him. "'Don't worry'?"

"Don't worry about payment. I'll handle your case on contingency."

"Meaning?" Ginger asked.

"Meaning, if we lose I get nothing but two new friends. If we win, I'll grab my ten percent, take some time off, and sail to St. Maarten with my guitar. Sound fair?"

Very!

"So Ginger," George said, smacking his lips, "where are those Grand Marnier thingies you were talking about? I haven't had lunch yet."

Two weeks later, our rock-and-roll lawyer surprised us with a visit.

"Well, guys, I got good news and bad news," George said. "What do you want to hear first?"

"The bad news," we said.

"I'm not going to St. Maarten."

"The good news?"

"Sonny Campbell is willing to settle out of court."

"Settle? What about a trial?"

"He's threatening to go belly-up."

"What does that have to do with us suing his ass off?"

"If Campbell goes bankrupt, we can't collect a dime no matter what you're awarded."

Our moan was almost musical.

"However, he's agreed to pay you twelve thousand dollars over the course of a year. I know it's just a fraction of what he owes you in every sense of the word, but it's something."

Twelve thousand dollars, minus George's well-earned contingency fee, wasn't anything to scoff at. After expressing our gratitude, we told him we were sorry that he and his guitar wouldn't be making sweet music in the Caribbean anytime soon.

"There's good news in all this," he said as he launched into an air-guitar solo, "I found me two new friends and rock star chocolates."

On yet another double-digit-dead day, we dusted each other off, watching office workers rush by our shop without a glance. In an ocean of debt, our monthly check from Sonny Campbell barely made a ripple in our checkbook. And, damn it, we couldn't even pull in customers with a winning lottery ticket.

Few things in the world were as dispiriting as throwing out stale chocolate. *Thou shalt not throw away chocolate* was probably carved into a chocolate tablet somewhere, but without customers, we had no choice but to commit that sin. It felt like we were going to hell.

Francie sighed into the checkbook. "No paychecks this week."

"What's with these Chocolate Scrooges?" Ginger griped.

"No one's in the mood to shop when the weather's this nice. They've all got spring fever."

"Playing Frisbee in the park."

Even if paychecks were a mere dream, a rich, little scoop of ganache—chocolate whipped with cream and butter—made everything better. Francie sliced a truffle in two and handed Ginger half.

"Thanks." Ginger slipped it into her mouth while glancing through the mail. Bills, bills, bills. "Hey, look, we got a card from Stella." She opened it and hiccupped with laughter.

A friendship card printed by the NA'AMAT organization where Stella served on board read, *Hope no one's giving you shit today. I'll be dropping by next week—I always save Chocolate Chocolate for my last stop. If I have to work til I drop, it may as well be with my two favorite gals. If we feel like it, we can get an early start on Halloween orders. Your dedicated servant, Stella.*

Taping it to the wall, Francie yawned. "Wish she was dropping by today."

A meeting with Stella was always a shindig behind the counter, and the fact that we got our candy orders placed between all our goofing off was a miracle. Inevitably she would end up waiting on customers like she owned the shop.

Stella reigned, but other vendors were good to us, too. Take Barry the Bag Man, whose family-owned company printed just about every bag toted around D.C. Barry was the sweetest guy around the Beltway and would often stop by to give moral support. Got a problem? Call Barry at Elman Labels. A compassionate guy, he extended our billing cycle—to infinity, he kidded—saving our necks month after month, knowing full well we'd pay him back when we could.

When neither friends nor chocolate could brighten our doom and gloom, sisterhood sustained us. Maybe our shop was splitting at the seams—for proof, we could look up to see decorative chrome peeling off the millwork—but not us, never us. Our stakes were too high: Without the store we might go our separate ways, and that was out of the question. We would pray for a miracle so hard it hurt.

~~

About a week later on a wet afternoon in late March, we were at it again—wondering where all the chocoholics were today. Francie knew.

"No one likes to go out and shop when it's raining. They're holed up in their offices."

"With their moody blues."

Just when we were feeling hopeless, the phone rang.

"Chocolate Chocolate," Ginger answered while nibbling on a particularly succulent piece of Dark Chocolate Orange Peel. She always searched good and long for the juicy ones.

"Yes, may I please speak to either Frances or Ginger Park?"

Her eyebrows stitched. "This is Ginger."

"Well, hello, Ginger. Jackson Jones here. I'm vice president here at Central Fidelity Bank over in Tysons Corner. My boss, Mr. Tomlinson, asked me to call you."

Ginger nearly choked up orange peel. We'd made the bank rounds in the city to no avail. But Central Fidelity was in the burbs. Where did this guy get our name, and why was he calling us?

"Yes, Mr. Jones?"

"Your accountant, Chuck Bandell, mentioned your new shop to the president here who, by the way, is quite the chocolate aficionado—his favorite is Thorntons from England. Anyway, we understand you're looking for a loan and we're hoping the two of you could drop by after work today."

Before Ginger hung up, we were busy making up twin chocolate baskets as if our lives depended on them.

"It was strange . . . ," Ginger murmured, arranging her goodies.

Francie, using Ginger's basket as a model, propped a candy bar up on a copper tin of chocolate-covered gourmet nuts. "How so?"

"Mr. Jones sounded so friendly, as if they'd be *honored* to do business with us."

"Well, they *should* be. But if they ask for collateral, we grab our baskets and run."

"Deal."

The highly decorous baskets we lugged up to the seventh floor of their office—one for Ed Tomlinson, the president, one for Mr. Jones—had them eating out of our hands.

"These look incredible," Mr. Tomlinson said. Then he sank his teeth into the biggest bonbon of the bunch, a Milk Chocolate Mousse Dream. Its swirly-whirly milk and white chocolate center made him dizzy and he sighed, speechless.

Mr. Jones comically rolled his eyes. "Excuse him, I think he just had a Calgon moment."

Side by side, we were in stitches, loving all bankers in the burbs—as long as they didn't sour everything with that one nasty word: *collateral.*

"That's too funny," we kept saying.

If only all meetings were like this, a heavenly aberration where all the stars seemed aligned.

"Frankly, we could sit here and eat chocolate all night, but I suppose it's time to get down to business," Mr. Jones said, moving the baskets aside to make room for paperwork.

Francie issued a silent prayer.

"My good friend and racquetball buddy, Chuck Bandell, put in a very good word for you," Ed Tomlinson revealed. "I would trust that man with my kids, so I trust you two will do fine in your chocolate endeavors."

Ginger crossed her fingers under her purse.

"Since he already supplied us with your financial statement, we went ahead and prepared our terms," he continued, handing us loan papers.

While the two bankers turned their attention back to their baskets, we pored over the papers searching for that one word. But . . . *no collateral!*

Afterward, the elevator ride down had the feel of a fairy tale.

"Guess who's getting the mother of all chocolate baskets?"

"Chuck Bandell!"

From a pay phone in the deserted lobby of the bank building, we called Mom. Yamagada cards shuffling in the background connected us to our only living parent, and with an out-of-control grin, Ginger cried into the phone, "Mom, guess what?"

"You got loan!"

"Yes!"

"I know so. Forty thousand dollar, no collateral, right?"

"Right . . ."

"See? My card never lie!"

Like puppets, our faces turned to each other: Mom's cards *were* always right.

Francie grabbed the phone. "Mom, how should we celebrate?"

"With pizza!"

We picked up a pizza from Victor's and rushed home, where the table was already set with a jug of Gallo and a pitcher of iced tea, three paper cups, crushed red peppers, and of course kimchi for Mom. A meal was never complete without kimchi.

Pouring herself a second glass of wine, Francie knew she wasn't making it home. In a way she loved a good excuse to spend the night in her old room, Ginger next door, Mom down the hall. Falling asleep here, safe in the knowledge that at least one bank had faith in us, made everything feel right with the world.

Chapter 8

Kahlua Truffle

A mud-black chocolate truffle
spiked with Kahlua
and dusted with cocoa powder

Warm weather brought out the soul of chocolate, made it deeper, darker, and creamier. The aroma alone drugged us, and in dreamy procession, three candy-buying occasions, each one a first for us, followed: Easter, Secretary's Day, Mother's Day. Like set designers, we learned how to stage our shop, make it gorgeous despite the flaws. For Easter, exquisite Italian chocolate eggs wrapped upright in brilliant foils that fanned out detracted from the mismatched tiles on the storefront columns. For Secretary's Day, metallic boxes encasing chocolate cameos brightened display cubicles that lacked the accent lights promised us. For Mother's Day, fancy "hatboxes" filled with pastel-foiled cordials were a perfect mask for all our scratched and dented shelves.

Business had been lively, but with the holidays over, the shop fell quiet again. How to pass the lazy summer days? With nothing but the heady aroma of the shop keeping us company, Ginger began daydreaming, and before long she had decided to convince Francie of her new idea, born from her sister's other dream which, after Dad's death, had all but faded: writing. In fact, when Ginger thought about it, Francie rarely spoke of her old raison d'être.

In elementary school Francie had preferred writing to recess, and in high school she spent her nights typing stories while her friends were at football or basketball games. After college when the editor in chief of *Ingenue*, a young women's magazine, called her with a dream job offer based on a batch of poems she'd sent the editor in the mail, Francie was all set to become New York's next literary darling. But the wintry day she moved up to the East Village, Francie received bad news: *Ingenue* just got word it was folding.

Already feeling the ill hand of fate, she applied for other jobs, including one at Brentano's Publishing. A series of successful Brentano interviews led to the Big One, and a final interview was scheduled. Unfortunately, it coincided with the blizzard of '78. While Francie sat in their waiting room, the interviewer, stuck in Connecticut snow, never made it into the city. Something felt wrong, all wrong. She ran out of the office and within days ran back home to Northern Virginia, as if something or someone was calling her. Dad's subsequent death meant only one thing: New York was never Francie's destiny. She had a different appointment to keep.

When the Chocolate Chocolate dream began to take shape and brighten our prospects for a life together, Francie's writing dream waned. But why should one dream eclipse the other? Balancing a five-layered tray stacked with Toffee Crunch Bars, Ginger approached Francie, who was wiping the already spotless glass of one of our display cases. She put down the tray.

"The other day," Ginger said, fingering the Yellow Pages on the counter, "I saw a listing . . ."

Francie stole the top Crunch Bar, made sure no one was looking, then began chomping away with pleasure. It wasn't one of her top tens, but it was there for the taking and sure beat crunching numbers. "Not for another lawyer, I take it?"

"No, for renting an electric typewriter."

"What?" Francie kept chomping. Nice and buttery, all munch and crunch, so good it just moved up a few notches on her chocolate-lovin' scale. "Why would we rent an electric typewriter?"

"So you could get back to your writing."

Writing? She set down her Crunch Bar. The notion of writing seemed so removed from the shop setting. "I couldn't write in here, Ginge, not with all the distractions. I'd need tomblike silence. Writing between customers wouldn't work for me."

"What customers? Francie, this place *is* a tomb. Can't you hear my *echo, echo, echo* . . . ?"

"Plus the fire's gone. I haven't written a word in a couple of years, at least."

"Maybe a typewriter will bring back the sparks. You never know."

"Spoken by my one and only fan."

Francie hadn't forgotten. Not long ago, Mom used to offer many a discouraging word. "My Fourth Brother was writer," she had told us a thousand times. "We call him 'noble beggar,' but when he die, he so poor, he leave hungry children."

Her Fourth Brother was the only one to survive the war. The first time we met him was in the summer of 1965 on a visit to Korea. He *was* a pauper, but who wasn't in postwar Korea? Maybe his writing dreams kept him alive while he and his children toiled in factories all day.

Still, after Dad died, Mom had a change of heart about Francie's aspirations. Two days before his death, Dad told her the day was coming when Francie would need their help and full support to fulfill her writing dream. He had gotten emotional. It was as if he had a premonition of his own death, knowing he couldn't be there for her, and hoped for Mom's nod. At least that was the way Mom would interpret the echoes of his declaration long after he was gone.

"Sparks, sparks, let's start some sparks!" Ginger said, air typing. "And I plan to get some use out of it, too. I've been thinking about writing children's books about our family."

"Really?"

And why not? Ginger had always loved children's literature, and Dad's death fueled a desire to unearth her roots and put them in writing with her own personal Korean-American stamp.

There were so many stories.

The hush of the store made the idea of a typewriter seem even more fitting. We rented an IBM Selectric for fifty dollars a month, a hefty sum for sisters who split coffee to save money. But somehow the investment, like Dad's premonition, felt right.

Taking turns, one of us at the keyboard, the other breathing over her, we test-drove our fingers and dove into action only to come up blank. Francie was rusty; Ginger didn't know where to start. The good news? We noticed a curious if not fantastical phenomenon right off the bat: Standing around waiting for customers was like watching a pot of water that never boiled. Customers wouldn't, wouldn't, wouldn't come in. But once we plugged in that typewriter and it began to hum, the doors seemed to open up more often—our first hint that indeed there *was* a whole city of people to get to know.

In between helping customers, we exercised our imaginations by typing out humorous vignettes based on some of the more memorable ones. Somehow, creating a story for the cast of characters that paraded through the store made us feel useful, and we certainly had more control over the page than how much business would or wouldn't come through the door.

There was

"Kahlua Lady," a self-made socialite, striking and elderly.

On her first visit, she told us she'd given up sweets long before we were born, but a serious chocolate craving had woken her up that morning.

"After forty-three years, I believe I'm entitled, right, girls?"

A tray of Kahlua Truffles caught her eye. Golf ball–size, dusted in cocoa powder, thick as mud.

"One, please."

Wasting no time, she bit off half, letting the cocoa powder fall where it may, all over her royal blue silk blouse.

"Oh, my, that was good . . ."

Now they were all Kahlua Lady craved, and she usually ordered a baker's dozen with one to go. Whenever she jet-setted, she told us, all she thought about were her Kahlua Truffles in the freezer and how long it would take them to thaw once she got back home to her Maryland estate—one hour. Her chauffeur, Geoffrey, made sure she was well stocked.

There was

"Dr. Zhivago," a tall man with wiry gray hair and beard, often in a Russian fur hat.

Nearly every afternoon, he would peruse our candy bar selection before choosing a dark variety and, as if to discourage dialogue, always paid with exact change. We respected both his stoic silence and nod when he left, all the while wondering: What was his story?

"Have a nice day," we'd say.

There was

"the Landlord," head of the alleged Evil Empire, a real estate magnate who owned not only
Oz but also buildings all over the metropolitan
area.

Already we'd heard so many horror stories about his company
mistreating tenants from everyone in town—industry associates,
other retailers, even customers. When he came in, we weren't surprised that he never smiled, introduced himself, or made eye contact with us. The outraged deli lady in the lower lobby said he
would bring his own bread from home, purchase only the meat
filling, and demand a sandwich discount.

"King of the Evil Empire," she'd spit.

From where we stood, in our dream space, he was simply the
Landlord—and, after all, he'd granted us our wish to be here.

"Have a nice day," we'd say.

There was

the dreaded "Bulldog," who was always barking
up his order for some stripper du jour.

We didn't exactly fight over who got to wait on him; indeed,
whoever saw him first either ran in the back room or got on the
phone, leaving the other at his mercy.

And then there was

"Our Girl Friday," whose face signified the
end of the working day to us.

Still enchanted, still catching the train to Philly, always breathless.

"Wish I could stay and talk, but as usual I'm running late! Have
a great weekend, okay?"

"You, too . . ."

As much as we looked forward to her visits, the fact that she was rushing off to her boyfriend often cast a lonely light on our own lives.

A rep at the candy show last summer had promised us that we'd have *all the men in Washington eating chocolate out of our hands.* Cool, but was she talking about *this* millenium? Sure, there were flirts, but these were guys who got excited over mannequins.

Marriage and motherhood weren't Francie's cup of tea, but she was ready for a little wining and dining—for the rest of her life, if possible. Ginger, on the other hand, would be happy just to find the perfect boyfriend.

No prospects on Saturdays, however. Since most D.C. workers lived in the burbs, the door never opened.

On the quietest days, we would add to our writing routine with fixer-upper projects in the store. Making our shop look nice without the camouflage of holiday merchandise was a challenge. Without her makeup, every imperfection stood out like a hairy mole. The chalky floors, the misaligned candy cases—*grrrr!* To gussy up our shop, Mom, the visionary who had turned sewing baskets into Valentine's keepsakes, began decorating plain, oval-shaped wicker boxes that we purchased wholesale from an importer in California. Much thought and decorum went into each oval, not to mention a Virginia Slim break or two. For the finishing touch, Mom nestled rosettes inside each one—chocolate ones, of course. Her ovals caused many an *ooh* and *aah.*

But no *oohs* and *aahs* on this Saturday in July, so hot the Reflecting Pool was at a boil. Only a handful of people had stopped in, and those just to cool off. Francie concluded that the prospects of even a double-digit-dead day were zero.

"No one wants to shop when it's this hot. They're zombies."

"Eating Popsicles instead."

Too dull to type, Francie blinked. "Let's go home."

"I was waiting for you to say that."

We were on our way out just as a bus pulled up. No ordinary Metro bus, its passengers were Japanese tourists—we recognized the foreign script on the bus.

"Why, look at that . . ."

At least once a week, Japanese customers—back then, always men—had saved our day by dropping fifty, a hundred, two hundred dollars with barely a sound. Point at a fancy box; hold up a finger count.

"Step away from the door, Ginge."

Ginger backed up, chanting, "Come in, come in, come in . . ." The bus doors slowly swung open. About two dozen young Japanese men tumbled out, scattering on the iron-hot streets. A trio headed our way, chatting.

"Francie, turn the lights back on."

Flick!

In they strolled, delighted to have found an American sweet-shop. Delighted yet no eye contact. True, we looked Asian, but a peripheral glance was enough to let them know we grew up on American rock and roll, and the cultural divide went up like a rice-paper partition. That said, we let them shop in peace. If offered help, they'd wave us away with their famous "Justa looking."

In the midst of excited foreign chatter, their eyes fell lustily upon Mom's ovals, strewn all over the store like Easter eggs. When they lifted a lid to discover chocolate rosettes inside, their chatter reached a feverish pitch. Each oval came with a price tag of thirty-five dollars, which apparently didn't faze them. Voices peaking, they began counting with their fingers. *Eight, nine, ten . . .*

"Thirty, please!"

Smart sisters knew better than to say a word and blow the sale. Just gather the ovals like flowers in a field.

"No, forty!" we heard.

Meanwhile, a second trio of Japanese bus mates came in . . . and then a third . . .

Forty ovals and eight bags later, the time had come to ring up the sale. Francie stood back just in case the cash register went up in smoke, and cleared her throat. "That's one thousand four hundred dollars plus tax."

Eyes smarting. "How much?"

"Including tax, one thousand four hundred and eighty dollars and fifty cents."

Pure slapstick: The trio shuffled a few inches, then formed a huddle. Our faces went from smiles to question marks, trying to figure out what was going on besides muffled chatter and bobbing heads. Then we heard the unmistakable sound of zippers in motion.

"Francie, are they . . . ?"

Gulp. "I . . . think so . . ."

Their huddle broke up and one of them thrust a thick wad of bills over the counter. Francie took it, knowing Ginger wouldn't. The money was warm and damp. But so what?

It was drop-dead-beautiful cash.

"Thank you," she said, handing them their change.

In unison bows, the Japanese men gathered their bags. "Thank you."

Klutzy but heartfelt, we bowed back.

"Thank you," we said.

As they were leaving, their bus mates began snickering in English, no doubt for our benefit. "*Sheesh*—farm boys!"

The next two sales were just as momentous yet not at all memorable. Everyone paid with American Express.

The following Saturday we hoped and waited for another Japanese tourist bus. Maybe Chocolate Chocolate was part of some new summer sightseeing package. But as the hours ticked by, we lost hope and grew tired of waiting.

"Guess we're not going to be on *Lifestyles of the Rich and Famous* anytime soon," Ginger said with a sigh.

While refreshing bowls of Italian hard candies out front—Isabella Fruits, Rosanna Eggnogs—something on the floor grabbed Francie's attention.

"What's that?"

A bird's-eye view from behind the counter gave Ginger a clear but not very pretty picture.

"The marble's cracking."

It was. With every inch of discovery, our hearts cracked a little more as we realized the hairline crack ran the length of our store from the front door to behind the candy case through our back room. We mumbled incoherently and gritted our teeth.

Gary Goldman, our second contractor, later explained to us that when the building was just a hole in the ground, the Landlord's contractor neglected to put in expansion joints before the concrete was poured. Barring a wrecking ball, it was too late. Already the whole building, most noticeably on the concrete garage floor, was riddled with little cracks. Now, whenever the weather got warm, Gary explained, our floor would expand and then crack a little deeper, along with our hearts.

Like unwanted trick-or-treaters, sometime around Halloween the Landlord's management team conducted an inspection of their retail tenants. Suits showed up at our door one morning like the Gestapo with their clipboards and phony smiles, taking notes and

mumbling among themselves, not even noticing our adorable chocolate pumpkins in the window. Days later we received a letter and
punch list in the mail from the Landlord, directing us to fix everything on the list or else we were in default of our lease. Number
eight on the punch list? The floor crack.

Turning on the IBM Selectric, we typed them a letter back
explaining that Gary Goldman told us the crack was *their* fault.

`    . . . And therefore, the Landlord is respon-`
`sible    for    fixing    the    crack,    not    us.`
`Sincerely . . .`

After that, they neither fixed it nor bugged us about it again.
But the Landlord's threatening presence and letter shed a crack of
ugly light: Maybe they *were* the Evil Empire.

Chapter 9

Devil's Dome

A wicked dome of dark chocolate

Every story has its villains, including ours, but there were good forces at work, too. Mom was a prime example. She had become more than just a parent; she was practically the shop's fairy godmother. Despite her support from the very beginning, her growing role in our business surpassed our expectations for one simple reason: Mom's nature was to retreat. As a rule, she rarely went out alone. She got her driver's license late in life, and while she knew how to drive, being behind the wheel wasn't a comfortable place for her, and it made us nervous, too. But over time, she had gotten into the habit of coming in with Ginger and working with us. Her cameo appearances seemed to liberate her from the confines of home and widowhood, and even her normally self-conscious English was "gone with the wind," as she liked to put it. And once in public, she inevitably made wallflowers of us. She endeared customers with her exuberance as she hurried from behind the counter to talk to them face-to-face, so close you couldn't say no.

"Hello! You are need chocolate today?"

With a trio of Parks in the store, it really felt like a family enterprise.

One morning in early December, Ginger came down with the flu. We had an appointment that day: Coeur de Chocolat was hosting a Chocolate Demo & Tasting for the public at Garfinckel's department store on F Street. Meeting the faces behind a product we promoted, especially one that was all the rage, seemed like a good idea at the time. But with Ginger bedridden, Francie would have to go alone. That morning she picked up Mom and they drove to the shop together. From there, Francie caught a cab to Garfinckel's, halfway across town.

Holding court with a big crowd of shoppers and reporters at the Garfinckel's tasting was a gentleman whose identity was known to most in the industry. He was Mr. X, president of the newly launched Coeur de Chocolat, poised to break all chocolate-sales records. From *Newsweek* and *Forbes*, Francie knew his bio: Formerly president of a multinational candy company and famous for the current gourmet chocolate trend in America, he reportedly left his previous employer on bad terms to start his own empire, and the two were now archenemies. When he saw Francie standing alone and looking rather lost, he waded through the crowd with a giant sparkling platter held high in the air like the headwaiter at a black-tie affair.

"Miss," he called out as he approached, "would you like some chawklate?"

A New Yawker.

"I've got it all here," he said, lowering his voice, and the tray, as he reached her side. "And they're all light as chiffon."

Francie laid her eyes on the tray, a lovely collage of chocolates sitting in gold scalloped candy cups. What to choose, what to choose? Her eyes fixed on a Devil's Dome, a wickedly dark little bonbon. Soon it disappeared from her fingertips, then from her lips.

Still savoring her sample, Francie met his questioning glance. Mr. X smiled, waited a moment, and then raised his eyebrows. "So, miss, how'd you like it?"

"Actually, I already know all your chocolates by heart." She laughed. "I'm from Chocolate Chocolate here in D.C."

"No kidding?"

"I know your name, too," she added.

"Oh, yeah? So why haven't you called me?" He offered her another Devil's Dome.

Back at the shop, Francie told Mom all about the meeting. Then she called Ginger, who was home, high on Nyquil.

Later that day as dusk fell over our shop, a flurry of customers danced in, spirits high, either from happy hour or the snow in the air, or some combination of the two. Whenever the doors opened, you could feel the snow, the magic, the witching hour. Anything was possible. Mom, back in her role, was bringing customers under her spell.

As the group left, a ray of hands went up: "So nice to meet you!" They were waving.

"You, too!" She waved back.

Presently, a black limousine pulled up to Chocolate Chocolate. Had Kahlua Lady's driver upgraded her town car? But instead of Geoffrey, a white-gloved driver opened the door for a well-dressed gentleman with jet-black hair. Francie recognized him immediately. Her heart began to pound as he made his way through the door. What was he doing here? Didn't he say he had a three o'clock flight to Dallas? For a split second their eyes met, but then the phone began to ring. It was Ginger, coming down from her Nyquil high.

Meanwhile, Mom was greeting Mr. X.

"Hello, sir!"

"How are you today?" he asked, towering over her.

"I do well, thank you. And you?"

"I'm fantastic. Beautiful shop!"

"Yes, my girls in charge here."

"I know. I met one of them today." He acknowledged Francie, just off the phone. "How are you?"

"Great," Francie replied, playing it cool and making introductions.

By now, two young intern types had made their way in and asked for change for the Metro while a businessman asked for directions to the University Club. Mr. X exaggerated a sigh that echoed the sentiment of many a shopkeeper. Francie shot him a small smile as she helped the businessman figure out the quickest route to his destination.

"Very nice to meet you, Mrs. Park," said Mr. X, turning back to Mom.

Mom murmured, not sure what to make of him, "You, too . . ."

"Say," he said dramatically, bringing a hand to his heart as he pointed out the sight of other chocolates sharing shelf space with his Coeur de Chocolat line, "I see you sell Neuhaus chocolates here."

"Yes," she confirmed, a bit suspicious. This man seemed successful though not distinguished enough for her taste. Not like her husband. Talk too loud, chuckling for no reason.

"Why, if I may ask?"

We often held "rehearsals" with Mom to prepare her for common questions. Q: Why did we promote Neuhaus when it was twice the price of other upscale chocolates in the country? A: Neuhaus chocolates were handmade, not machine made like those others. Despite our coaching, Mom always delivered her own translation.

"Neuhaus hand washed," she explained as if he was the biggest idiot on earth, "others machine washed."

Like Times Square at night, Mr. X lit up. "Mrs. Park, you're beautiful."

Overnight, Mr. X was the man in Francie's life. He flew her up to New York, where a limo was waiting to whisk her to his many-mirrored apartment on the Upper East Side. He flew down for a night and they stayed in the Hay-Adams, where they ordered room service and never left the suite.

Francie, the ingenue chocolatier; Mr. X, the chocolate legend. He knew everything she didn't, and that impressed her. Attracted her. Mr. X was a glamorous figure, the older man with unmistakably boyish charm.

"So," she asked him over champagne and little plates of exotic food as Christmas lights flickered outside his window on East Eightieth Street, "exactly how old are you?"

"Just like the media reports, I'm forty-nine, Miss Chocolate," he replied. "What's it to you?"

Mr. X liked to keep it light at all times, at least with Francie. His serious side he kept for nonstop business calls, which were either very loud or very muffled and often heated, taking place at all hours—on his couch, in his bedroom, even in his bathroom where a phone hung next to the shower. Francie was always Miss Chocolate to him. Mr. X spent half his life in Europe, usually Paris. Whenever a French operator called with a person-to-person call for Miss Chocolate, Francie got a tingle, as if she'd stepped foot in the City of Love without leaving the shop.

Secretly, Ginger wondered if he thought calling her sister by her real name would feel too intimate or committed. She didn't approve, and her disapproval was creating a crack between us, as ugly as the one running through our floor. United on every front, we were always Laverne and Shirley, two for one, until now. Ginger had met Mr. X once when he popped into town unannounced and despite, or perhaps because of, his over-the-top charisma, she didn't trust him. Her big sister had made some questionable choices in the past, and several had been considerably older, but not Mr. X old, and Ginger would exhale with relief whenever things went kaput. She saw Francie as a girl divided—with her wildly romantic side and her bookish side—and always felt the latter was the true person, though the former was winning this time.

One day at the shop, Ginger just couldn't hold her tongue any longer. "Francie, why are you dating him?"

"He's fun and exciting, that's why. And get this—he flies his own planes."

"I don't believe that. Besides, he's an old coot."

Francie let out a rather reckless laugh. "Sometimes you just got to live out things, Ginge. It's not like I want to marry the guy." What was wrong with having good times with someone who could show you things in this world? Help you. "You should try to like him, a little, or at least not hate him. Look, he's placed free ads in the *Post* for us."

"And you sleep with him! People will think you're a gold digger."

"Oh, please, Ginge. He's not rich."

Although he did wave that corporate American Express card around like he owned his company.

"By the time someone's as old as him, he *should* be rich," Ginger said. "You know, Mom doesn't like you dating an old coot, either."

When Francie scheduled overnight trips to see Mr. X, she likened it to chocolate, a guilty pleasure. "Let's talk about something else." She changed the subject as a fortyish gent with blue-blood airs stormed in.

"Pardon me, let me catch my breath." He huffed and puffed, his red silk bow tie no match for his fuming face. "Before I waste my time, I need to know something: If I give you my Christmas list, can you handle sending out gifts to my clients and friends, or is that just too much to ask?"

When we assured him we were here to make his life easier, he drew a relieved breath and an explanation for his frustration. "For years I did my business with Berry Pretty in Middleburg, but they went out of business, such a pity . . ." His eyes drifted over to the tray of White Almond Bark, all nutty and glistening. "So I went to the candy department in Garfinkel's, and they were rude to me. Rude! They just didn't want to be bothered. I guess they had better things to do. I guess they just didn't want the business."

"Well, *we* do," Ginger assured him, wrapping up a generous slab of White Almond Bark for his immediate pleasure. "Here you go."

The gift took him off guard. "Why, thank you!"

"Say," Francie ever so politely queried, "what's your name?"

Despite this gentleman's old-money aura, there was something curiously accessible about him.

"Edgar Hewett," he replied. "I'm with E. F. Hutton up the street." He glanced at our business cards on the counter. "Francie and Ginger, very nice to meet you," he said, reaching into his pocket. "Now, here's my Christmas list. I'm not sure you'll be able to read my scribble, not sure at all."

His twenty-odd-page list of clients, family, and friends was a directory of who's who in Washington, D.C., along with a smattering of mature heiresses who lived in the best parts of Georgetown and Kalorama. His elegant penmanship was from epochs past.

"Oh, Edgar"—Francie came around and took his arm—"have we got the perfect gift box for you."

For us, Edgar's Christmas list was already a sign of prosperity that ended the season and kicked off a new year, 1985. Inaugural events soon tinged the frigid Washington air, and excitement was building.

Still, it wasn't unusual to find us milling around behind the counter like monks. Better to keep quiet than argue about Mr. X. The chocolate gods wouldn't like that. It was all a little weird. Whenever somebody strolled in, we both jumped up to offer our help.

Certain things brought us back together, if only for the moment.

Like a call from a customer informing us that we were mentioned in the *New York Times* that day, listed as a shop in the nation's capital not to be missed by inaugural visitors. Rushing out the door without her coat, Ginger raced over to the newsstand on K Street, dodging traffic and couriers on bikes. When she returned, we opened the *Times* to page A20 and stood over the paper, each of us holding it open, breathing, not moving, our fate lines one and the same.

"'The Boutique Clique Hits Town,'" Francie read the headline aloud, "'The inaugural visitor . . .'"

We couldn't believe it. We were finally getting somewhere, cracked floors and all.

Obviously, we weren't the only ones who saw the article, for soon the phone rang again. The voice on the other end was female with a sniffy accent. "Yes, I would like to speak to the owner, please."

"I'm one of the owners," Francie replied. The voice was vaguely familiar.

"This is Marie from Maison d'Or. I have heard all about your shop in Washington, D.C., and—"

Francie motioned to Ginger to pick up the other line.

"Did you say Maison d'Or?" We exchanged a look.

"Yes."

"And were you at the Fancy Food Show last summer? At their booth?"

"Yes."

We exchanged another look. "Okay," Francie said, "go on."

"We would like to discuss with you our most exclusive chocolates. Maison d'Or is very selective, you know. To shops that meet our very high standards, we offer a full sampling program and free freight over a minimum opening order. Have you ever tried Maison d'Or?"

"No, I never got a chance."

"Well, we must change that, young lady. Our product is far superior to Manon of Brussels who charges outrageous prices for mediocrity. Would you be interested?"

"Oh, *most* interested."

"How wonderful!"

"There's just one problem."

"Certainly not price point. In Washington, D.C., you have an international clientele that would gladly pay a hundred dollars per kilo for Maison d'Or."

"Oh, sure, we have plenty of rich customers. *Plenty* of them. The problem is . . ."

"Yes? Yes? What is the problem?"

"You don't sell to our kind of shop."

"*Pardon?*"

"That's what you told us at the show."

"*Mais non*, I am sure there was a misunderstanding."

"Oh, I'm sure there was, on your part. And you want to know something? We wouldn't sell your chocolates if you gave them to us free."

Marie aka Madame Skunk had no recourse but to apologize for what she claimed was certainly a misunderstanding. "My English is not so good and—"

"Neither was your perfume," Ginger said stonily.

"Pardon?"

Slam!

A double slam!

More fun than any inaugural ball, we doubled over in laughter and a hard high-five.

Sisters again.

Chapter 10

Cashew Turtle

Cashew-studded caramel smothered in chocolate

But soon, a solo sister act once again, Ginger opened up shop. Even the shop felt different when we weren't in sync. *Click, flick, sigh* . . . Francie's six-month thing with Mr. X (well, you couldn't call it a real relationship or even a fling, he was too *old* for either, in fact, you couldn't even call him a boyfriend, give me a break, not at *his* age) was still on. How many bottles of Grecian Formula did the guy go through a day to keep his hair that black? He claimed to be forty-nine, but, c'mon, the man looked too old for Mom. A sugar daddy; no, a sugar *grand*daddy, the way he lavished gifts upon Francie, a cashmere robe from Milan and perfume from Paris. Suddenly, on a pauper's salary, Francie was a gift giver herself, buying him man trinkets from Raleigh's, a cigarette lighter, a pair of cuff links, as if she owed him something. Well, the guy must be waving some magic wand because Francie was definitely under the spell of his brash jingle: *I always get what I want.* And what he wanted was Francie to move to Manhattan and join Coeur de Chocolat, as if *our* company didn't count. The nerve! What would half of Chocolate Chocolate be without her?

Just Chocolate?

Speaking of which, it was time to replenish the trays. Arranging chunks of peppermint bark—big ones on bottom, little ones on top—a whiff of chocolate menthol went up her nose. Soothing. Medicinal. On the radio, the Temptations were singing about sunshine on a cloudy day. The harmony of chocolate and soul music was downright prescriptive, even without Francie.

Speak of the devil, here she was, an hour late, fresh off the Eastern Shuttle.

"Hi, Ginge!"

"Hello."

"By the way, you were right about his age," Francie said, bringing up Mr. X immediately, as she fluffed her hair in the back-room mirror. "I peeked at his passport when he was in the shower—he's *fifty-three.*"

"Must be a fake passport."

"Why do you say that?"

"Because he looks *eighty*-three!"

Our chortles were all we needed to get our day back on track. For now, Mr. X fell off the face of the earth while we fell back into a familiar chocolate song and dance of straightening up, fiddling with the radio dial, and joking with anyone meandering in on this warm day. There weren't many. Despite the nod from the *New York Times*, sales, we were learning, were hard to sustain off-season.

A month passed and it didn't surprise Ginger one bit that her sister's Big Apple soirees were becoming less frequent and less charming. She'd stumble in vacant eyed and go quietly about her business. Francie's love affairs always had a shelf life, but Ginger had a gut feeling something was speeding up the process. Something amiss.

"How was your night in New York?" she asked.

"Fine." Francie bit her lip. "I guess."

"You sure?"

"Yeah."

Ginger could see the writing on the wall: It was only a matter of time before Francie dumped Mr. X. And who could blame her? Mr. X was so creepy the way he called up the shop on his speakerphone asking for Miss Chocolate, please. Don't you know she has a name? Francie needed to open up, and there was only one way to do it.

Ginger dug out four whopping Cashew Turtles—two milk, two dark—so heavy they nearly bent back the tongs. Then she chopped them into bite-sized pieces and laid the gorgeous chocolate-caramel-nutty mess on a white paper doily.

"Breakfast is served," she said.

Stan the UPS man was dropping off a small carton when he caught one of Francie's idiosyncrasies: her prelude of long desirous looks before taking the first bite. With a smile, he told Ginger on the way out, "Your sister doesn't eat chocolate, she seduces chocolate."

"God, Ginge, these are *sooooo* good," Francie pronounced like she was famished for so much in life. "I really needed this."

"I thought so. What's going on with you and—*cough*—Romeo?"

"Eh." She shrugged. "He's being sued by another company and then there's apparently all this in-house fighting at Coeur de Chocolat. It's weird, the company's going public, but it's also for sale. And some recent article about him in *Barron's* was the death of him, or so he says. I don't really know what's going on, but it sounds bad."

"Go on," Ginger said, munching away.

"And then there's his paranoid personality. Early on, it was kind of fascinating to me, somehow, like seeing the main character from a novel unfold. Everyone, he swore up and down, was either spying on him or stealing from him or conspiring against him, everyone from his investors and partners to his employees to his longtime, about-to-retire Portuguese maid."

Ginger rolled her eyes. "His *maid?*"

"He'd say things like, 'Now that she's leaving the country, she's hoarding my silver. But I'll get even, don't worry, I have a plan for her.'"

"What a nut."

"Even his closest friends became suspects, people he planned to squash at their own game, although they'd never guess it from his phone chuckling. 'Jerry, old buddy, old pal, how's the most famous cookie maker in Manhattan?' He doesn't trust a soul, Ginge, not even me, I'm sure."

Because he can't be trusted, Ginger was thinking.

"Lately, with all his ranting and vendettas, he doesn't seem so fascinating anymore. Especially since he didn't even bother to read the folder of short stories I left him. I poured my heart and soul into them and he's too busy tallying up how many silver spoons are 'missing.' Every time I see the untouched folder sitting on his dresser, I flinch."

"How do you know it's untouched?"

"I put a penny on it."

Ginger bit her tongue. Her sister's heart and soul weren't worth a red cent to him, rat that he was. Still, this wasn't the time to rock the boat. This was time to keep the chocolate peace. Gobbling up the last few crumbs of our chocolate breakfast, Ginger felt like a girl in braces again, a mouthful of chocolate-caramel-nutty mess sticking to her teeth. "Well, it sounds as if high finance mumbo-jumbo made him paranoid."

To Francie's nod, Ginger sighed, relieved to be in agreement. We lived and breathed for this one little shop, on this one little corner. Whew, it was nice to feel in sync, even if only for a moment.

The phone rang and Ginger picked up. "Good morning, Chocolate Chocolate."

"Miss Chocolate, please."

Usually when Francie got on the phone with Mr. X it sounded like a block party in the back room, but Ginger couldn't hear anything this morning. When Francie came out front, she spilled the news. "Coeur de Chocolat filed for bankruptcy."

Ginger shrugged. The company had produced an unquestionably fine product and we'd built up a loyal following for those who craved their chocolates with a lighter touch. The problem was Mr. X. "Oh, well," she said unconvincingly.

"And that's not the worst part."

"I thought that was the *good* part."

"His investors have locked him out of his own office and refuse to reimburse him for all his business and travel expenses, six months' worth. They're shutting down the company and leaving him high and dry."

"Not our problem," Ginger said.

"No, but he's helped us out—"

"How?"

"For one thing, he's given us cases of free stuff."

"But was it his to give?"

Francie paused. Maybe not. The whole thing was so confusing. "I want to help him. I feel like I owe him."

"What are you talking about? Help him how?"

According to Mr. X, unless his investors reimbursed him for his American Express bills, his credit would be ruined, and he was defined by his credit rating. How else would he start up a new company?

"He's still got access to the Coeur de Chocolat warehouse and has arranged for the boyfriend of an employee to pack up some merchandise to eventually sell to department stores. Some department store bigwigs have agreed to pay him personally for the chocolates."

"Steal, you mean. Not pack up."

"Take what's his. He's owed the money."

"Whatever. It's none of our business anymore."

"Actually, it is, Ginge."

"Why?"

"Because I told him he could warehouse the merchandise in Mom's basement. It's already en route."

Our conversation was put on hold as a crowd of Capitol Hill staffers dropped in to arrange deliveries to the Hill.

But after they left: "He's got a thousand places to store stolen chocolates," Ginger cried. "Why at Mom's house? And did you ask her?"

"I already called her, and she's fine with it. You're the only one who isn't."

"Does she really understand what's going on?"

"I explained everything to her."

Ginger's sarcasm was loud. "Yeah, I can just hear your explanation."

"Look, when he was on top of the world, he was good to us. Why have you hated him since day one?"

"Because he's a thug in a fancy suit, that's why. He's manipulating you!"

"That's ridiculous!"

"You should wash your hands of him and never talk to him again!"

"You know," Francie said, "maybe if you found your own boyfriend, you wouldn't be obsessing over mine!"

"Think what you want, but I'd rather be alone than with the god of Grecian Formula!"

We didn't utter another word to each other all day. Maybe if we'd broken out the Cashew Turtles again, a chocolate peace would have fallen over us and we'd remember why we were here in the first place: our shop. However, neither of us had an appetite, so we carried on like zombies, putting on our happy faces for customers only.

At six o'clock, after the cash registers were settled, Ginger usually dropped Francie off at her apartment. But that night, she watched her hail a cab on Connecticut Avenue without a glance back.

Back to the solo-sister act. She closed the shop. *Click, flick, sigh.*

In the cab, Francie felt horrible about what she said to Ginger about finding her own boyfriend. It was so out of character. What would ever drive her to say that?

Her thoughts turned to Mr. X, and she tried to think about what was happening. Essentially, he was looting his own store, and if that was the case, he was using her and her family as unwitting accomplices.

Before her coat was off, she called him from home. Maybe Mr. X was a man who always got what he wanted, but that was about to end.

"Miss Chocolate! How's life in your provincial little town?" He loved to insult D.C. as if there were only two cities in the world that mattered: New York and Paris.

"Take the chocolates back," she said. "Tomorrow."

He hesitated. "Why?"

"Because I'm not going to be a smokescreen for you."

Suspiciously: "Why the change of heart, Miss Chocolate? Is it because your sister hates me?"

"I never said that."

"Leona Helmsley's sweeter to me than your sister. Is she the reason you—"

"She's got nothing to do with it."

"Well"—he took a calculating pause—"does Miss Chocolate need me to explain better why I need her help and in return, how I can help her and her family? Because believe me, you want to keep the chocolates there."

Was he threatening her? Her business? Her *family*?

"Don't tell me what I want," Francie warned him, controlling her rage. "Just get those chocolates out of my mother's basement by tomorrow afternoon, or Miss Chocolate's throwing them out."

Mr. X was still talking when Francie simply said, "I'm done with you," and hung up.

For her, the breakup didn't hurt a bit. But her argument with Ginger kept her up all night.

The following morning she called Ginger. "Can you pick me up today?"

Confused: "Sure . . ."

"Tell Mom the chocolates in the basement will be picked up this afternoon. We're not storing them after all."

Hesitant: "Okay . . ."

"And, by the way, Mr. X is history."

Later that morning we zoomed into work, up I-395 and over the Memorial Bridge, at a loss for words. Still, for some reason, we didn't feel like turning on the radio. The Potomac River below seemed especially blue and expansive, as if we'd just woken up from a long, dreary winter's dream and realized it was summer, splendid summer. We focused on the cheerful image of food carts lined up off Constitution Avenue across the monument grounds. They'd probably always been there, and we never noticed. Today, one stood out.

"Look, Ginge," Francie said.

The food cart was shiny as a silver dollar. No wonder. While his parents were preoccupied with food preparation, a young Asian boy was rubbing a rag into its steel exterior with all his might.

"He's so adorable." Francie stared as we drove by. "But what's he doing downtown?"

Ginger frowned. "He should be at the pool, playing with other kids."

"Such a hard little worker trying to please his parents."

"Like Dad."

As a thirteen-year-old growing up in the outskirts of Seoul, Dad went to work as a milk boy before and after school in order to help feed his starving family. Rising long before the sun, he would milk goats, then balance milk bottles on a rusty old bike and pedal into the city to deliver them to wealthy Japanese families and merchants. That some people drank dirty water while others drank milk would affect Dad long after those mornings of pedaling through the moon-lit dark.

Something about seeing the boy at his family's food cart broke the ice between us.

"Ginge, I'm sorry about yesterday. You know I didn't mean what I said."

Ginger didn't look her way. "Sure."

"Seriously, you have your pick of eligible bachelors."

"Like who?" After all, there was only one Rafael.

Emceeing the D.C. *Dating Game*, Francie cleared her throat

and spoke into an air mike. "Bachelor Number One attends one of the finest private schools in the country and leaves love messages for Ginger on our answering machine . . ."

"He's also fifteen years old," Ginger pointed out.

"Bachelor Number Two is Washington's famed French chef who hand-delivers you teeny tiny raspberry tarts and lovely lemon mousse concoctions in the hope of a single kiss."

"Fat and married," Ginger sang.

"Can't forget Bachelor Number Three, a powerful lobbyist known to spend more time in our store than on Capitol Hill."

"Once more, not a bachelor and bald to boot."

When Ginger grabbed Francie's air mike and tossed it out the window, we laughed so hard we nearly wrecked the car.

Habitually during our commute we found ourselves on the lookout for the little boy. Our eyes skipped over all the other food carts and zoned in on the shiny cart and, in our minds, a fretting family. They never seemed to have any customers. We both worried: "What will become of him?"

One morning, stopped at the traffic light, we spotted him helping his parents unpack plastic eating utensils. Francie squinted, trying to make out the print on his T-shirt.

"Aw, his name is Mike."

Ginger, with her twenty-twenty vision, laughed. "That says Nike, Francie!"

"Well, he's Mike to me."

After that, every morning as our car approached Constitution Avenue, we would ask each other, "Where's Mike?" until our eyes found the boy who had unwittingly helped us make up.

It was easier to worry about Mike than ourselves. The good news was that our second Christmas at Chocolate Chocolate we had to hire part-time college girls. The holiday was so busy that when it was over, we hardly had the strength to carry our deposits to the bank. Yet after all was said and done, after we paid all our bills, there was little left over. How was it possible we still weren't making any money? The only bright moment of the entire season was when Chauffeur Geoffrey showed up unexpectedly on Christmas Eve day. We were confused, as Kahlua Lady hadn't called with an order.

"Hi, Geoffrey, did we miss the memo?" Francie wondered.

"No." He laughed, holding up two presents in metallic wrap. "Mrs. Powell wanted me to give these to you ladies."

They were matching black umbrellas with brilliant butterfly designs, delicate and exotic, meant for a walk in the rain in the tropics. The card read, *Francie & Ginger, I saw these and thought of you. Merry Christmas, Kahlua Lady.*

"They're beautiful," we cooed.

Her gift and recognition of her nickname made our year.

Chapter 11

The Bouchon

Tiered cognac-flavored ganache,
crème fraîche, and hazelnut praline,
sprinkled with edible gold flecks

Building up a close-knit clientele with the likes of Kahlua Lady worked wonders. It helped keep at bay what seemed like our fate: to struggle financially for the rest of our lives.

Thank goodness for Fridays, when our cash registers got a workout. That was the one day of the week people felt like they deserved a treat. Even grumps who dismissed our shop with a glare on Monday were looking in and smacking their lips. And one particular Friday we got the feeling everyone in Washington was feeling entitled.

It was January 17, 1986, and people were marching our way like armies of ants from Connecticut Avenue, north and south, and both escalators in our lobby, up and down. Unnerved, we asked each other, "What's going on?"

The first group in was a boisterous bunch and let us in on the secret.

"Look," said a woman with a big glossy auburn bob, "you're in the *Washington Post* today." She held up the Weekend Section so we could read the cover headline: "Indulge Yourself."

Delighted to be the bearer of good news, the woman handed the paper to us. "Read on," she said.

"Where do you find the single best bonbon in the city? At Chocolate Chocolate . . ."

The bonbon in question? The Bouchon from Manon of Brussels. Hah, Madame Skunk was wrong about Manon. Perishable and so costly we ate only the ones that got crushed in shipping, their offerings were distinguished by tiers of pure chocolate, crème fraîche, praline, amaretto, marzipan . . . But the most sublime was the Bouchon, a triple-tiered goddess of bittersweet ganache, vanilla crème fraîche, and milk chocolate praline. The top tier was double-dipped in chocolate, doused with cognac, and sprinkled with edible gold flecks that made your eyes glitter. And the experience of devouring a Bouchon?

Pure chocolate wattage.

Lips were smacking. "So, where are they?"

"Over here." Francie enticed a shop full of eyes to the middle candy case where we illuminated our most pricey, if not prized, confections.

The parade of new customers in our door continued, even though by midday we'd sold every Bouchon in the house. Buzzed with optimism, we were swapping remarks behind the counter while we were boxing chocolates and ringing up sales.

"Let's go shopping this weekend. I need a new handbag . . ."

"Maybe we should pay Barry the Bag Man back first . . ."

"Aw, but Barry said it was no hurry . . ."

"Well, I do need some sunglasses . . ."

～

It took us two years to settle our debt to Barry the Bag Man, but, in our defense, those two years passed quickly. Faces came and went with the seasons, and the days passed in a blur. There were trying times, but in memory it was sweet, all sweet, including our celebration with Barry when we finally wrote him the last check. Happy, he treated us to dinner at Rumors on M Street.

Like chocolate enchantment and customers waving whenever you looked up, some things you could count on: Our Girl Friday, like clockwork, keeping her standing appointment; Kahlua Lady sweeping in for a box of her cocoa-dusted favorites with one to go; bow-tied Edgar strolling in every year with his Christmas list, adding names here, crossing off names there; Dr. Zhivago studying our candy bar rack, mysteriously mum as ever. Other things were less predictable: realizing one morning that the Asian family's food cart was gone—*Where's Mike?* we'd lament for a long time; the death of Goldie, our sweet pup who hopelessly waited for years for Dad to come home; the crack in the floor getting deeper and more ragged.

Now that Mr. X was a distant memory, Francie began dating again, often a customer who loved chocolate as much as her. This meant there was always something to talk about if the conversation went south or got halfhearted. But more and more of her heart belonged to her fiction, something she could count on to love, a pen in one hand, a bittersweet nut cluster in the other. Behind the candy counter with Ginger, dalliances on the IBM Selectric continued, but at night, writing was a serious matter.

Ginger spent her evenings with Mom, watching television, and then, after Mom went to bed, curling up with a notebook full of scribbles and story ideas centering around a character she called the Milk Boy. But, like her love life, nothing materialized. Falling asleep, she'd wonder if there was anyone on earth for her, or if those few hours with Rafael were all life was giving her. Maybe if they had stopped walking that night, went into a bar and had a drink, that would've changed everything. Maybe they would have settled down together. But they didn't. So a single look, a single night, a single memory all added up to this: a single girl in the burbs.

It was time to stop thinking about what his Baci love note said, she told herself. Crumple up Rafael's memory like the foil wrapper it came in. Done!

While living with Mom was a godsend for Ginger's bank account, not to mention the spicy Korean food always bubbling in the kitchen, a part of her longed to be closer to D.C., in Arlington or Georgetown where all the action was, where people her age hung out at clubs and cafés. Wouldn't it be fun to have a boyfriend who would take her to places like Filomena and Bistro Français? Well, it was nice to have a dream. No wonder most Saturday nights Ginger could be found home baking fancy cakes from cookbooks, tortes and gateaux, though once she mastered their cheesecake-marbled decorum and frou-frou raspberry liqueur drizzling, she realized that plain chocolate-on-chocolate cake ruled, hands down. The only way it would taste better was if there was someone to share it with.

Still, a part of Ginger was happy where she was. Besides, she couldn't leave Mom alone in the house night after night. Were Dad alive, our parents might be at the movies or out to dinner—their "dates" had become more frequent as the kids grew up. Indeed, their last few years they acted like honeymooners. But Dad wasn't alive, and though she could never take his place, Ginger knew Mom needed her.

"Ginger," she would often tsk, "why not you should go out on date? You too picky."

"I'm happy here, Mom."

Which, for the most part, was true. She loved watching Mom

lost in a glass of wine or a screwdriver, smoke swirling from her Virginia Slim while she waxed on about her life in long-ago Korea. No matter where the stories began, they always ended at the same place with the same lament: "I never see my mother again. Not know what happened." This was the central theme of Mom's life, what drove her sadness. Dad died long before his time, but at least she knew how he lived the last days of his life, and that they were good ones.

"I really am happy here, Mom."

Living with Mom wasn't a sacrifice. These were precious times. Someday she would look back and be happy that they had these mother-daughter moments, something Mom never had with her own.

Speaking of precious, the growing intensity of the knockout smell of chocolate could mean only one thing: warm weather was here and Easter was around the corner. Our shop was transformed into a wonderland populated by hundreds of chocolate bunnies, big and small, hopping about in the midst of pastel ribbons, grass, and tissue. There were little imported eggs of liquid caramel and strawberry sugar crème snuggling happily nearby old-fashioned American eggs the size of your fist. Jelly beans were strewn everywhere; the traditional fruit pectin beans as well as the gourmet Jelly Bellies popularized by President Reagan in mouth-watering flavors such as Strawberry Daiquiri, Banana Split, Sour Apple, Piña Colada.

So come on in.

Feel five years old again.

Unpredictability made shop life fun, as there were only two givens: We never knew who was coming in and every day took on a life of its own.

Despite the warmth of the decor inside the shop, our double doors had been installed out of joint, which made cold, windy days a nightmare, as one door never completely closed, leaving the shop frigid, not to mention they were arthritic and equipped with subpar hinges. Fortunately, today was glorious out, and just as glorious was Lulu's beaming smile as she maneuvered her way inside. Nothing confined Lulu, especially when she had a hankering for dark chocolate Coconut Baron Bars. In theory, a cross between Almond Joys and Mounds bars, they were made with the good stuff, and it seemed like Lulu would travel over mountains for her fix. No easy feat, as she was in a wheelchair and this was long before the Americans with Disabilities Act made its way into law. Still, Lulu always managed to seem both unstoppable and unfailingly cheerful— hence her nickname, Ms. Gratitude.

"Sorry about those wretched doors," Ginger said with profuse apology as she held them open for her. We always tried to help Lulu, though customers often beat us to it.

"No problem." She laughed. "But I keep telling you not to do that, Ginger. One of these days I want to look up and see my Prince Charming holding the doors open." Her wheelchair rolled over the crack in our floor and she laughed again. "I keep forgetting about that speed bump."

Meanwhile, Francie was busy wrapping up a chocolate bunny in pale yellow tissue paper for a woman who was talking about her grandkids in Ohio. The bunny was so big Francie could hardly manage it. She appraised her work. "Ten pounds of pure milk chocolate."

Departing, Lulu delivered a quick whisper to Ginger. "I'm sorry, but if it's not dark chocolate, it's just not chocolate."

A guy outside opened the door for Lulu, looked in with a stunning smile, then walked by, waving.

"Babe alert, babe alert. He's waving at you, Francie!"

Francie looked over. "Who? Where?"

"There!"

The mere image of this blue-collar guy with surfer blond hair caused beads of sweat to collect on her neck. But the juvenile bounce in his walk made him seem too young for her.

"He's still waving, Ginge . . ."

"Then wave back!"

So Francie granted him a little wave, which seemed to satisfy him—for now.

As the lunch rush was dying down, Gypsy Bess flew in. A divorcée of sixty-three with so much to say she would gasp in midsentence, she was a bohemian gal defined by her floppy jewel-embellished hat and swinging beads as she skirted through the lobby toward our shop, not to mention her energy. She loved only one thing more than her feminist literature: chocolate.

"I'll take two of my precious Chocolate-Dipped Apricots today. Make that three, Ginger—my doctor told me to lose twenty pounds, but I told him 'diet' is a four-letter word. I'd even give up sex before chocolate," she unabashedly stated for the record, "if I *had* it to give up!"

Poor Gypsy Bess. She loved her ex-husband, Joe, but not enough to accept his philandering ways (we'd heard the whole story). Four years before, she divorced him, emerging feistier than ever. The next year, with the backing of the National Organization for Women, she became a cause célèbre in the media for pressing charges against her boss, a state politico in West Virginia who expected her, as his secretary, to babysit his son. Two years ago, Gypsy Bess packed her bags and moved to an old high-rise just south of Old Town Alexandria, a place she'd never been to but always romanticized, and found a secretarial job over on K Street. Last year, not knowing a soul here, she had found and befriended us.

"We had a good marriage for twenty-five years, but Joe's wandering eye went too far," she said with regret, removing her floppy hat and setting free a mad cap of platinum curls. "How much, darlin'?"

"Two dollars today, Bess."

Francie was out front, primping up displays, when Ginger psssted with another babe alert.

There he was again, the Babe, walking by and waving—Francie's heart skipped a beat. She waved back, but Gypsy Bess came first.

"With your ex's wandering eye, it's kind of ironic he's going blind, isn't it, Bess?"

Gypsy Bess sadly dug into her treat—life was too short to resent someone forever, even if he did break your heart. "Joe always loved to sculpt, but losing his sight probably ruins it for him, Francie. Oh, you should see some of his work—I have some pieces in my apartment. You girls are still coming over on Sunday, aren't you?"

Bess was the first customer we had socialized with on the weekends, and the fact that a deep friendship had formed beyond the mere customer-shopkeeper dynamic made us feel as if Chocolate Chocolate was slowly becoming what we always hoped it would.

"Of course we are," Ginger said, rolling a sheet of paper into the typewriter and loving its hum. It was the sound of keeping another dream alive. Just as she started to plunk away, Bill-About-Town bounced in. He was always on the go, an outgoing and sprightly guy with a red beard and, today, a sky blue Hawaiian shirt.

"It's Bill!"

"It's Ginger!"

An author and literary agent of nonfiction, he was also a pilot, a photographer, a wine tour guide, and who knew what else. It seemed to us that he had his hands in many pots, and they all turned to gold. On his agenda today: Milk Chocolate–Covered Pretzels.

Grinning, Ginger assumed, "Your usual dozen?"

"I'm going on a long road trip, so better make it two."

As Ginger opened the case and bent down to fill his order, she heard him whistle: "By the way . . ."

She poked her head up. "Yes?"

"Ever hear of a word processor?"

Meanwhile, Gypsy Bess was leading Francie into a corner, just outside the back room. "'Chat Corner' time."

The Chat Corner was a little space where time stood still. There was nothing really special about it except the air created between two people beneath a recessed bulb that flickered like candlelight. And here was where Francie and Gypsy Bess's friendship bloomed. Indeed Francie seemed able to open up more to Gypsy Bess than anyone else she'd met in a long time.

"If the weather's good," Gypsy Bess was saying, "I'll pack us a chicken salad lunch and we'll wander into Old Town and eat on the river. Is your mama coming?"

The two had met the month before at Mom's birthday brunch over at Francie's place and hit it off right away. Although Mom had loved Bess and had a grand old time, she ventured out only now and then. Getting her out again so soon was unlikely.

"No, I don't think so."

"Come on, Francie, twist her arm."

"She's not outgoing like you, Bess."

"Well, I'll pack an extra lunch, just in case. Oh, and afterward I'd love for you girls to meet my friend Juanita, who owns a vintage clothing boutique on Princess Street, then take you over to the Torpedo Factory where we can gawk at the art."

"Hey," Francie was reminded, "did you ever get around to signing up for their art lessons?"

"Not yet. I haven't picked up a brush since my divorce. All I'm good for is finger painting."

"You're a women's libber, so liberate yourself. Just take the plunge."

"You're right, love. And speaking of liberation, when are you going to show me your stories? My nights are free and I want to read them, each and every one of them."

Francie paused. You could confide in someone face-to-face, but writing was a different kind of personal.

"Someday," she said.

After work, the Babe was leaning against the stair rail in the lobby. He'd been waiting for Francie, and she knew it.

"I'm Darren," he said.

Maybe we'd attracted a new regular.

Chapter 12

Pecan Chewy Bar

*An impressive slab of caramel
capped with chopped pecans, then
dipped and drizzled in milk chocolate*

In a restaurant overlooking the Potomac, Francie got a closer look at Darren and realized that his sun-kissed hair had fooled her. From a distance he looked twenty-five, but close up, more like thirty-five and a bit weathered, though for some reason you could never picture him growing old.

Darren tipped his wineglass to the waiter. His signal for "two more" morphed into a lovey-dovey peace sign.

"Soon as I saw you," he said, "I had to meet you."

"I'm flattered," Francie murmured, drunk with attraction. She wasn't the only one. Half the women in here were looking over, probably wondering what he saw in her.

"I love your face. Can I call you that?"

"What?"

"Face."

She shrugged. "I guess."

A pretty boy from the wrong side of the tracks, Darren spent his days supervising a construction crew, and his IQ wouldn't break any records, but in a strange way, Francie found it refreshing to be with someone who carried himself like he didn't have a worry in the world. Still, she thought, no way would their relationship go beyond tonight. Darren loved fast cars and wished eastern shore living was a full-time job—the water, crab shacks, cracking open beers.

"What do you do for fun?" he asked.

"Write," she said, half hoping that would turn him off. Then she could be on her way with no regrets.

"Cool." He grinned. "Tell me about it."

She did, for a good fifteen minutes. Darren surprised her by being a decent listener; wineglass in one hand, chin in the other.

Still: "Word of warning, Darren. I'm no beach bunny, so we probably have little in common, you know?"

"You're not getting rid of me that easily." He laughed. "Besides, I come with a warning myself."

No joke. "Oh, yeah?"

"I don't like being alone."

"Well, who does?" Francie lifted her glass, and they toasted to it.

Later that week, during a lull in the shop, we were goofing off and filling up trays of assorted bonbons.

BANG!

"What was that?" Francie cried.

Ginger looked out and made a face. "It's one of those damn

couriers parking his stupid bike against our glass. I'm going out there to give him a piece of my mind."

"I don't know, Ginge." Francie stared. "Look at him. He looks like someone on the FBI's Most Wanted list."

The courier in question, unscrewing a water bottle cap and taking a long drink, could've just stepped out of Woodstock with his wild Abbie Hoffman hair, a coal black mustache, and a red bandanna so ratty he should've left it in whatever dog's mouth he ripped it from. Only a pair of wire-rim eyeglasses and a slight paunch spared him. Okay, so maybe he read a book or two in his life. Still, Ginger wasn't impressed.

"He doesn't scare me," she said, halfway outside. "Hey, you, do you mind moving your bike? Why do you couriers think you can just lean your bikes on our property?"

Hmm, close up the guy was actually cute.

The courier squinted at her, followed by a laugh. "Francie, don't you recognize me?"

Confused, Ginger squinted back. "I'm not Francie."

"You're not? Then who are you?"

"Are you drinking bong water? I'm her sister Ginger."

"Oh, my God, you're kidding!"

"No," Ginger said drily.

"Sorry, but I haven't seen her since college. Our old friend Carol told me about the chocolate shop. So I was riding by and thought I'd say hi."

By now Ginger was putting pieces of the puzzle together. Carol was Francie's roommate from college, the two used to hang out with a guy named—

Francie stuck her head out. "Skip, is that *you*?"

"Hey, Francie, how ya' doin'?"

"It's been ages."

The next thing Ginger knew, Francie and her old friend were dancing a reunion bump as if "Do the Hustle" was playing on a boom box—a strange sight considering it was 1988 and they didn't have a disco bone between them. But the college buddies did party together during that era and now something was coming back to Ginger: She had met this guy before and thought he was cute then, too, in a Cheech and Chong way. Yes, Skip and her crush at fourteen were all beginning to feel very déjà vu.

While Francie showed Skip into the shop and the two got reacquainted, Ginger was recalling one long-ago Friday afternoon in 1976 when she unexpectedly showed up at Francie's apartment at Virginia Tech, having caught a ride with the older sister of a gymnastic buddy.

"Surprise!"

It was a surprise, all right. Francie looked shocked, and not necessarily in a good way. In retrospect, maybe college girls didn't like hanging out all weekend with their kid sisters in braces and Keds.

"What are you doing here, Ginge?"

"I came to see you. Aren't you happy I'm here?"

"Well, sure I am, but . . . why didn't you tell me you were coming?"

"I wanted to surprise you."

"Oh, that's great," Francie had said airily, trying to be nice. "Only thing is, there's a party tonight. Carol and I know the band and, well, I've just got to be there."

"I don't mind waiting here for you," said Ginger the innocent. Of course she was hoping they'd spend the whole evening together like when she popped in unannounced the year before. They'd waited in line to see *All the President's Men*, then headed over to

Carol Lee's Donut Shop where they sat on stools and watched throngs of students pass by. "I brought some magazines with me."

"No, no, we can't have that," Francie said, plotting something. "I have another plan."

In no time, Ginger was all dolled up in platform sandals and a killer yellow halter top with white frilly straps. She bore little resemblance to the girl who had knocked at the door two hours earlier.

"My work is done, and it was devilishly fun," Francie sang, painting her nails hot pink with glitter—she wasn't going to be outdone tonight. "You look old enough to get into any frat party."

Once there, she warned Ginger, "Please don't open your mouth, okay?"

"Why not?"

"If you blind anyone with those braces"—she sipped her punch, studying the crowd—"they'll know you're underage."

The band was obviously not the main attraction for her big sister, Ginger could tell: Francie was hoping a certain someone would show up tonight. His name was Jeff, an elusive boy who made her heart flutter. But alas, he wasn't at this party.

Instead: "Skip!"

"Hey, Francie, how ya doin'?"

Back then with his hair squeezed into a ponytail and a mustache bigger than his face, Skip would've scared a Hell's Angel. Mocking disco, the two greeted each other by launching into exaggerated versions of the bump.

"Where's Carol?" he was shouting above the party noise.

"Somewhere!" she shouted back.

Afterward, Skip noticed Ginger standing in the shadows.

"And who, may I ask, is this gorgeous thing?"

Ginger did everything to keep her lips sealed but she broke into a silver-gleamed grin. *He called me gorgeous!*

"She's not a *thing*, she's my sister Ginger. And she's fourteen, so hands off, old man."

"Fourteen? Wow, you could've fooled me!" With that, Skip deposited both his and Francie's drinks in her hands. "Here, hold these for us. We're gonna hit the dance floor."

"Now, don't drink them," Francie warned as she pranced off. "I'll be right back."

Watching them dance, Ginger got a little curious about the cups of punch in her hands. She inhaled. They smelled good, like Hawaiian punch. Just one sip. Mmm, really good. One more sip. She got giddy, thinking about how this Skip guy called her gorgeous. Another sip. Soon both cups were empty and she stumbled to a chair in a dark corner where she promptly passed out, baring braces for all to see.

"Oh, sorry. Ginge, you remember Skip from Tech, don't you?" Francie said, rushing the introduction because Dr. Zhivago had just slipped in. Even though our customer wasn't a talker—perhaps he spoke broken English or none at all—you got the feeling he liked to be acknowledged. She greeted him with a nod.

With a yawn, Ginger gave Skip the once-over. "Looks like you lost a ponytail and gained a gut."

Skip grinned. "Gee, nice to see you again, too. If memory serves, you got pretty tipsy that night in Blacksburg," he said.

"No thanks to you two," she defended herself. "And believe it or not, I haven't had a drink since."

"Seriously?" he said, checking her out. "Because you're definitely legal now."

Francie remembered seeing Skip at happy hour many times, many years ago, at a college bar called Mr. Fooz, circled by girls for reasons that went right over her head. Now, his old come-on was making her wince. Signing for a delivery from Stan the UPS man, Francie quipped, "Watch it, that's my baby sister you're talking to."

"There's nothing babyish about her anymore," Skip quipped back.

Francie rolled her eyes, setting down the package. "Oh, brother, Skip, you look old enough to be her father."

Rearranging packages on his hand truck, Stan interjected, "*Grand*father."

Amid this, Ginger's heart was pinging off the walls.

"Want a tour of the shop?" she asked Skip.

"Sure, but can I say two things?"

He was going to say he was married or engaged or gay. Ginger braced herself for the worst. "Yes?"

"First off, I'm not a courier."

"Okay."

"Second, I heard your father died a few years ago. I'm really sorry to hear that."

Ginger was touched. Not only was he still cute, he was genuine.

"Thank you," she said.

Whatever charm Skip exhibited two minutes ago went the way of a candy bar wrapper when he cast his critical eye on our beloved boutique, all pretty and frilly with Easter candy. He didn't spare any criticism on the flaws that, after four years, our eyes tried to skirt over. The whole Sonny Campbell story was old news now and bored us to tears.

"This place is a wreck," he kept mumbling. "Why don't you re-place these shelves? They're so beat up."

Ginger bristled. How dare he carry on like this, like he owned the store? Look at him on his hands and knees, checking out every nook and cranny with a judgmental frown.

"What happened to your floors?"

"Excuse me?" Ginger said, hands on hips. "Look, we didn't come this far and work this hard only to hear you cutting down our shop. Wipe that frown off your face."

Skip, like some perfect store cop on duty, was too busy muttering to himself to hear her. "This store looks a hundred years old . . ."

"Skip's not actually frowning," Francie said.

"He's not?"

"No. Unless he's grinning ear to ear, his droopy mustache makes him look depressed. In college, Carol and I used to think Skip was suicidal until we realized it was just his 'stache. The longer it got, the deeper his frown. We called him Eeyore."

Our sisterly howl went on for a good five minutes. Francie failed to keep a straight face while she waited on two ladies looking to put together an Easter basket.

Skip cracked up for no reason. "Hey, are you two laughing at my expense?"

Ginger retorted, "Most people compliment, not criticize, our store!"

"Well," Skip said, "I got a compliment for *you*."

Ginger blushed.

Although we played music all day, it was often drowned out by distractions. But there were times when the perfect song came on at the perfect time, and this was one of them—"Blue Moon" by the Marcels. *You saw me standing alone . . . without a love of my own . . .* Ginger waited, waited for the compliment while Skip looked down, searching for the right word.

"I think you're incredibly . . . *Oh, my God!*"

"What?" Incredibly Oh-My-God what? Gorgeous? Sexy?

"Look at that crack in the floor!" he cried.

After a brief summary of our construction woes, Skip, uninvited, came behind the counter and offered to try to help conceal the unsightly crack.

"I'm not saying I can erase it, but with a little putty and caulk I can level it out and make it look a little better."

"Sounds very Revlon," Francie joked, still helping the two ladies collect goodies for their basket.

"Skip," Ginger said, secretly pleased that he was coming back to fix the crack, "since you're an old friend of Francie's, you can pick out any one single piece of chocolate. On the house."

He shuffled. "I don't really have much of a sweet tooth."

Ginger doubted a bachelor in his thirties had a delicate appetite when it came to candy, ice cream, beer, or anything else.

"But," he wavered, "since you're treating, that Pecan Chewy Bar sure looks lonely."

The Pecan Chewy Bar was a fat three-inch-long slab of vanilla caramel capped with sweet chopped pecans and dipped in rich milk chocolate. The whole thing was drizzled in more chocolate, and if that sweet brick of heaven didn't satisfy you, nothing would. With only one bar on the tray, Ginger let him take the last Pecan Chewy Bar with his fingers.

"Wow," he said, chewing like he could chew forever, "got any more of these in the back?"

For old times' sake, Francie and Skip decided to go out for a drink after work. Ginger declined, insisting on closing up shop alone so they wouldn't miss Thursday happy hour.

"We can get you a Shirley Temple," Skip teased her.

"No thanks," Ginger said, not wanting to be the third wheel.

"C'mon, Ginge," Francie begged her. "Don't worry, we won't leave you with our drinks again," she joked.

Ginger's smile was firm. "You two have a lot of catching up to do. Next time."

After settling the registers, Ginger turned off the lights, plopped herself on the metal stool, and watched the Washington working world pass her by.

"So, did he say anything about me?"

The next morning at the shop, Ginger wouldn't stop hounding Francie, who was surprised by her interest in Skip. Rafael, he wasn't. But apparently his enigmatic sex appeal lived on.

"Well, did he?" Ginger asked. Again.

"My messy daughters need maid," Mom proclaimed, scrubbing our white hand sink spotless. No matter how hard we scrubbed, we could never get it to sparkle the way she did. Maybe Mom inherited the genes of ancestors who washed laundry on rocks in the river. Such a notion would make her scoff with conceit because, in ways, once a rich girl, always a rich girl—even though she would scrub down the whole store without complaint. Well, it was something to do. Her frequent cameo appearances of late meant her days were uneventful with Goldie gone.

"Yes, Ginge," Francie caved, "Skip asked about you."

"Details, details."

In a rushed, run-on sentence, Francie reluctantly replied, "He said you were cute and asked if you had a boyfriend and I said no but you probably weren't available."

"But I'm available every hour of every day and every day of every week and—"

Protective Big Sis interrupted. "You two would be ridiculous together. Besides, he's not really boyfriend material."

"Why not?"

The phone rang with Kahlua Lady calling for her usual. Chauffeur Geoffrey would be by around noon to pick up her treats.

"My trip to Greece was ruined, Ginger," Kahlua Lady reported. "Forget the baklava, forget the *kataifi*. We took a ferry to the Cyclades Islands, and the only thing I could see through my binoculars were my truffles. In Andros my husband broke the news to me—quite sheepishly, I might add—that he'd polished off my truffles before we left D.C. Imagine that! And with our staff on vacation while we were gone, the whole time I knew I'd be coming home to an empty freezer."

"Poor Kahlua Lady," Ginger joked along with her. "You sound like you're on the brink of a nervous breakdown."

"If I don't get my favorites today," Kahlua Lady told her, "hospitalize me."

Ginger said good-bye, then began to prepare her order. She opened a box, laid down tissue, and grabbed tongs. Before long, it was back to Skip.

Francie sighed, wiping beneath the scales where chocolate crumbs always collected. "Look, in college, it was a different girl every night."

"I remember Skip," Mom chimed in, recalling the time he came knocking on our door with Carol to collect Francie for a night out in Georgetown, many summers ago. "He seem smart like Russian scientist, but why he wear flip-flop in my house? Man in flip-flop not dignified. But he seem okay."

Gypsy Bess was winging in with her morning coffee, delighted to see Mom. They embraced like long-lost sisters. Mom's imperfect English and Gypsy Bess's mile-a-minute chatter had them speaking a language no one else could understand.

Afterward, Gypsy Bess turned to us. "Your mama's so beautiful."

Mom blushed. "No, you are."

"Bess," Ginger broke up the party, "I need some advice on love."

"I'm neither Aphrodite nor Ann Landers, darlin', but I'm all ears and I'm all yours. Shoot."

Mom returned to straightening up shop. Enough talk, talk, talk when there was work to do. Besides, she'd heard all this gibberish before.

"Francie doesn't like the idea of me going out with her friend Skip," Ginger explained.

"Why not?" Gypsy Bess seemed surprised. "Francie, don't you want your sister to go out and have some fun before she's an old broad like me?"

Francie was blunt. "I just don't want Skip to think of her as a one-night stand, that's all. Frankly, I'm not sure he'll appreciate how special she is."

"Sweet girl, I love you more than life itself," Gypsy Bess declared, "but here's my column of the day: Ginger should have some lovin' in the bubble bath with whomever she wants and come out of it with a memory for every bubble, good or bad. Everyone warned me about Joe, but I was in love and I married him anyway, and you know what, girls? I'm glad I did. I have my memories and four beautiful children, and I'll always love Joe, or at least a part of him. Go for it, Ginger—that's my advice and I'd syndicate that advice to all the women I love," Gypsy Bess said before flying off and calling over her shoulder, "I'll be back after lunch for my apricots."

"See, Francie?" Ginger pleaded.

In some ways, we'd always be Big Sis, Little Sis.

In the end, Francie conceded. After all, it was Ginger's life, not hers.

"Cool," Ginger said, watching a limo pull up outside the shop—Chauffeur Geoffrey. "That is, if I ever hear from Skip again."

That Saturday night, Ginger was trying her hand at making toasted almond toffee. If successful, she planned to lightly coat her toffee pieces in a velvety wash of milk chocolate. After years of baking on Saturday nights in the burbs, she was a master baker, but this was altogether new territory, and toffee is tricky. Tonight's candy making was to be kept a secret from Francie, who would turn Ginger's toffee into their shop's signature bonbon before the sticky goo even hardened. Take out all the fun.

"Save some for me," Mom was saying in the background, shuffling her Yamagada cards. "Cards good tonight, Ginger."

Ginger hummed happily. Maybe that meant her toffee would turn out perfectly after all. Melting butter and sugar over medium heat, she stirred all the while with a big wooden spoon, watching, waiting, for the candy thermometer to rise to 275 degrees. This was the crucial moment in the toffee process; one minute or one degree off and the butter-sugar mixture—not to mention her mood— would burn.

Naturally, the phone rang. Well, it couldn't be Francie, who'd mentioned something about going out again with Darren—he'd been in the shop every day since their first date and had already pet-named her "Face." As babelicious as he was, it was curious that her sister would put down her pen for a guy who, judging by his interest in quitting hour and Budweiser, probably never read a book in his life. Then again, he *was* dangerously good-looking, too hard to pass up.

Ginger heard Mom answering the phone. "Oh, yes, who is calling?" Pause. "Okay, just for second." Mom called out, "Ginger, phone call!"

There are three key rules in order to create a toffee with the perfect snap and crunch: (1) Keep an eye on the candy thermometer; (2) constantly stir; (3) never leave the stove.

"Take a message, Mom. I'm busy right now!"

Mom appeared in the kitchen and whispered, "He say he Skip."
Without thinking, Ginger dropped her wooden spoon and raced to the phone. Breathlessly, she picked up.

"Hey, Ginger, it's Skip. How ya doin'?"

There was something inherently funny about Skip and it was hard to say whether it was his mustache or simply that he was Francie's friend. But something about him gave Ginger license to tease him. "I'm doing just fine, Eeyore."

Skip took his old nickname in stride. "I'm glad I caught you at home. I figured all the guys would be knocking down your door on a Saturday night."

"They are, but I have better things to do."

"Yeah? Like what?"

"Like making homemade toffee, for one thing."

"Wow, sounds like a pretty wild scene."

"Quit making fun of me and maybe I'll save you a piece."

"Like I said, I'm not much of a candy eater."

"Judging by that belly and the way you hogged down that Pecan Chewy Bar, I find that hard to believe."

His hearty laugh made her smile. "Ginger?"

"Yes?"

"How about me taking you to brunch tomorrow? I can pick you up, say, around noon?"

"Well . . . ," she said, so excited she could scream, "I guess so. But listen, I've got to go. I just realized something."

"What?"

"My toffee's burning!"

At the brunch buffet at the Front Page in Dupont Circle, Skip seemed more starved for talk than food. After some casual banter, the

conversation took a serious turn. Skip admitted that he had just
ended a serious relationship and was casually dating other women.

Red flag.

Maybe Skip wasn't the person Ginger would spend the rest of
her life with, but she was enjoying the moment with a mimosa in
her hand, her first drink since that infamous evening at Tech.

"I just haven't been passionate," he said, pushing his eggs Bene-
dict about with his fork, not making a dent.

"About women?"

His mustache flipped up. He was about to say he hadn't been
passionate about his work but decided to play along. "Yeah, until I
met you."

Ginger blushed, fourteen all over again. "Let's take it one moment at a time," she said with a toast.

He toasted back. "Your chocolate shop's the coolest spot in town."

"Thanks. I guess you can tell we got off to a rough start, but
we've managed to make the best of a bad situation."

"Francie told me where your seed money came from. Your father
would be really proud of you."

Green flag.

She smiled. "So what about you? Where do you work?"

Skip had taken a sabbatical from his job as a contracted health
physics technician for nuclear power plants all over the country and
was now earning his master's in radiation science at Georgetown
University. Once he completed the program, he hoped he could
find more stable work, perhaps at the National Institutes of Health.

"I fell into my job right out of Tech. It was perfect for a while. I
was young, single, and got to see the whole country. But I don't
love my work like you love chocolate."

Ginger nodded. Despite still struggling to make a decent profit,
she loved chocolate more than ever.

After just one brunch date, it seemed that Ginger and Skip were inseparable, and all of Skip's other women fell by the wayside. When Skip wasn't at school or studying, he was hanging out at the shop with us, and soon his crush on gourmet chocolate rivaled his crush on Ginger. "I'm starvin', Marvin!" he would say as he reached for yet another hunk of almond bark. And it wasn't just chocolate that turned him on; he was charmed by the whole entrepreneurial experience. He envied us for having the one thing he never had: a dream. Our enthusiasm as proprietors and our dynamic with customers made his own career track seem dull, and he found himself growing increasingly bored with radiation science. As a result, Skip became a pretty regular fixture around the store.

"Is this Peanut Butter Brontosaurus Egg for real? It's like eating a chocolate football."

"Skip," Francie teased him, "there's no law that says you have to eat it all at once."

Skip's toolbox became a regular fixture as well, as we asked him to make repairs on a daily basis. Being our personal handyman wasn't the dream of a lifetime, but he enjoyed it. Not only had Skip expertly disguised the growing crack in our floor, he also built shelves along both walls of our back room, transforming a cluttered shoe box into useful space. He replaced our dented chrome shelves with warm glass ones. He installed track lights in our storefront windows so that come evening, a biblical glow settled on our displays. Every half hour without fail, his head would pop up.

"Is it chocolate time yet?"

Despite his critical eye and Eeyore traits, we loved having Skip at the store. From day one, it felt preordained, like he was destined to drive us crazy for the rest of our lives.

As Stan the UPS man quipped one afternoon, "Fran, it's time

you changed your name to Mary Ann. Ginger and Skip have fallen for each other hook, line, and sinker."

Holding the door for Stan as he maneuvered his hand truck onto the street was a young man, dark haired and striking. Francie stuck her head in the back room where Ginger and Skip had started putting away a shipment.

"Ginger, Ginger, there's someone here to see you."

Ginger stepped out only to feel her heart stop, then flutter. Even though she had put him out of her mind, the dizzying memory of a single night four years ago had survived. It was Rafael, handsome as ever.

He smiled.

She smiled back. "Come back to buy more Bacis?"

"No. I came back for Ginger-in-a-candy-store."

"What?"

"I'm living on Capitol Hill now."

"Oh, Rafael . . ."

"Don't tell me you're married," he said.

"No," she uttered, not quite sure what she was feeling. Had she never met Skip, Rafael could bring it all back with a single look: their walking, their talking, their silhouettes cast under the streetlamps. And she couldn't help herself; a part of her was still dying to know what that Baci love note said. That single message. Asking him was on the tip of her tongue. Instead, she swallowed hard. "But I do have a boyfriend now."

Boyfriends aside, Saturdays remained sister-to-sister.

Sometimes Ginger would pass the time at the typewriter. *Plunk, plunk, plunk* . . . Stuck on the same story, she couldn't progress much farther than its title, "The Milk Boy." Thankfully, Ginger had Skip to distract her from the frustration of writer's block.

Francie's own distraction was Darren. It made no sense, considering he smoked, drank too much, and happily suffered from Peter Pan syndrome, proud of his cartoon watching and speeding tickets. In a million years he couldn't discuss Nabokov or Isaac Bashevis Singer or Graham Greene, her literary gods. But they had fun and he relaxed something in her. He could massage away all the kinks. A paradox. Darren, enamored with her writing dream, set up her apartment with a desk and a word processor and presented her with a Waterman writing pen that cost him two paychecks. He had only one request: "Don't leave me alone at night, Face."

At the shop, Francie might glance at whatever story she was working on, but after hours she buckled down in the privacy of a closed-off room, not anywhere near the television in the next room where Darren could often be found. She hadn't sold any of her short fiction yet and showed her stories only to Ginger and Mom, her little fan club. Yes, even Mom was on board now. Francie's correspondence with editors indicated she was getting close, very close. Placing a story with a literary magazine was her dream.

"Any day now," Ginger kept assuring her. We got into a comforting rhythm: the two of us manning the store each day, Francie splitting her time between Darren and her writing. Ginger and Skip off to play tennis on Sundays. But just as we had our sights set elsewhere, we were faced with a very different kind of turning point.

One sleepy Saturday in the fall of '88, Skip was interning at the NIH but God knows he would rather have been with us, making a coffee-and-bagel run or tackling another discovered defect in our shop, masked by baskets of foiled chocolate leaves. A rustling sound in the back room snapped us out of our dreams.

"What was that?" Francie said.

"Skip must've gotten off early," Ginger said, getting up and heading to the back. "Skip?"

When the door jammed, she tried to push it open but was shoved out of the way. Too paralyzed to react, we heard a shuffle, then saw a young man in a black warmup suit dash out of the back room, out our door, through the lobby, and onto the street.

"Stop!" we yelled ridiculously, feeling sick to our stomachs.

We'd been robbed.

In the back room our wallets were lying on the floor—exposed.

"Our money's gone," Ginger said, sinking on top of three big plastic bags of trash. "So much for going to the mall tonight."

"What about the money tin?"

Ginger dug behind the bags and found the tin on the floor. She shook it, heard money, grew hopeful, then opened it. Our petty cash and Friday's banking were still there. Good thing we'd been too lazy to clean out the back room that morning.

When Skip got to the shop, he nearly had a coronary when he saw us filing a report with two police officers. He ran to Candey Hardware, with two realizations: It was time to put a lock on the back-room door, and it was time to put his studies on the back burner. Three credits short of his degree, he dropped out of Georgetown to join the business. How mad was that? He and Ginger had been dating only six months.

"I can always go back to school next year. Right now your safety's at stake. Besides"—his mustache twitched—"I kind of like it here."

So two became three.

~~~

Who wouldn't like it here? Chocolate Chocolate was always a magic box, especially at Christmas. Step inside and stay forever. One morning when the shop was perfumed with bittersweet mint chocolate topped with green-as-a-dream colored sugar—complimentary nibbles—a young man with a fetching grin walked in. His face didn't ring any bells, though he seemed to know us somehow.

"Hi there, can I help you?" Ginger inquired, as always.

"I have a hunch you can," the guy said.

"Great!"

"You know," he began melodically, "I've heard quite a lot about the famous Park sisters."

Except between ourselves, we were hardly famous.

"From whom?" we asked him.

"Heather Hall."

No bells.

He knocked his head. "Ah, she said you know her as Our Girl Friday."

"You're the Beau from Philly!" we both cried.

Yes, and he was hoping to soon be the Husband from Philly, he explained. "I was wondering if I could buy one of those little boxes she brings me every Friday."

Ginger plucked one from a display basket. "You mean this diamond ring–sized box?"

Pleased, the Beau from Philly pulled a tiny blue velvet jewel box from his coat pocket. Then he flipped open the lid to reveal a ring as glittery as Our Girl Friday.

"Think it will fit?" he asked.

"Perfectly," we replied.

At closing hour, Our Girl Friday rushed in.

Francie played dumb. "What are you doing here? It's not Friday."

"Oh, come on, David told me you know all about it," she said, barely containing her glee. Flashing her diamond ring, her voice fell with emotion. "Ladies, this is the happiest day of my life."

"Congratulations," we both said.

"We're *so* happy for you," Ginger expressed.

"I'll be moving to Philly next month. It's not that far, and I'm sure I'll come down to D.C. once in a while. Still, I'll really miss you two. My little ritual certainly didn't help you stay in business, but it meant a lot to me. I want you both to know that."

The truth was, her little ritual probably meant more to us. We met Our Girl Friday early on, when every face was a stranger to us, when most days, even the good ones, had their hollow moments. Expecting her breathless dance in the door every Friday kept us going. The minute we came around the counter to hug her, she was anchored in our memories.

Then Our Girl Friday vanished onto a crowded sidewalk where a row of streetlamps gave off a sentimental glow.

It felt like the end of an era.

Chapter 13

Monster Mint Patty

*Cool mint cream encased in
bittersweet chocolate*

Indeed, time would usher out the Reagan era along with every chic boutique around us while a camera shop and shoe palaces moved in. One of the restaurants on the terrace level in our building had closed, and rumor had it the other one was feuding with the Land-lord. So our building, once Oz, had lost a bit of its luster but not Chocolate Chocolate. By the early '90s we were actually the only original shop still standing and, in fact, a couple of storefronts had been boarded up unleased.

The new era also had Francie egging Ginger on again to create a signature chocolate. One, just one. Like that Willie Nelson song, that elusive chocolat de vie was always on Francie's mind.

"It'd be so special," she insisted.

"Shhh, don't let Skip hear you or I'll never hear the end of it,"

Ginger warned her in an exaggerated whisper. "Besides, why would it be so special?"

"Duh. Because you made it."

Though Ginger's stance hadn't changed, the face and the pace of downtown had. We saw fewer minks and more Patagonia, fewer three-piece suits and more khakis. Friday was now casual day, and most office workers conducted business in blue jeans. More important, with our vision limited to our shop, we saw fewer workaholics and more chocoholics. Customers lingered longer, in no hurry to get back to their offices. Some would invite us to step out for lunch, but since sales were up and we were finally profitable, at least one of us had to stay with Skip to man the shop. A coin flip determined who got to go.

Everything felt more down-to-earth. Not only that, we could each afford our own cup of morning coffee now.

Chocolate culture was changing, too, and the beauty of our business was that we could change with it, making more room for extravagant European pralines or humble Wisconsin fudge, however fickle our love. When *Washingtonian* magazine had bestowed a "Best Of" award to our Naron Milk Break-Up Chocolate, beating out the competition at thrice the price, we expanded our local offerings with six new trays of clusters, nougats, and buttercreams. Suddenly, the old-fashioned line of chocolates was in, and the whole town understood what we'd been saying for years about our Baltimore chocolate maker: Eating their candy was always a happy walk down memory lane.

Ms. Gratitude was in and Skip was waiting on her. By now he was expert with candy tongs, though helping customers wasn't really his forte unless they were talking chocolate *and* politics. Our politico in residence, he loved to talk the ears off of anyone willing to listen to his views. That aside, Skip preferred being behind the scenes in the back room where he'd built a small desk, responding only to our urgent knocks on the door signaling Bulldog's presence—now we made Skip deal with him. More number-oriented than us, Skip did away with our eyeball record keeping and established an accounting, ordering, and inventory system. But waiting on customers and being on show out front was not his preference. If he wasn't in the back room, he was usually at Au Bon Pain—his disappearing acts were famous.

"Well, I don't care if it won a *Washingtonian* award, milk chocolate's for the birds." Lulu was an out and proud chocolate snob. "Might there be such a thing as a *Dark* Break-Up?"

"Right over here." Skip pointed to the tray on her far left. Though a bit shy around customers, he went out of his way to help someone in need, sometimes too much. "Can you see it? Over here where I'm pointing?"

"Of course I can see it, Skip. I'm not blind."

"Sorry, ma'am."

"And please don't call me *ma'am*. I mean, do I *look* like somebody's grandmother?"

"No, ma'am."

Lulu cracked up. "Francie, where'd you find this boy?"

"He's not mine, Lulu."

Ginger laughed. "He's mine. We were married last year."

While most brides to be planned for the most important day of their lives, Ginger had dismissed all formalities. She wore a simple white silk dress, held a homemade bouquet, and with a simple "I do" in front of the justice of the peace at Mom's house, she married Skip. Without Dad to walk her down the aisle, what was the point of a lavish wedding ceremony? As it was, his absence filled the living room.

Initially the couple had rented a tenth-floor apartment in

Arlington with glassy views of the city. The place was glam but cramped with pots and pans, cookbooks, bicycles, and tennis equipment. A tight fit. Yet it felt empty to Ginger, especially knowing Mom was alone most of the time. Even though at least one of us went over to have dinner with her every night, seeing her face in the window when we drove away was heartbreaking. Soon enough, Ginger and Skip decided to move into Mom's house.

When Mom learned that Skip had been born on June 26, 1954—the *exact* same day our parents arrived in this country—she knew it was a fated union. Needless to say, Mom and Skip formed a unique bond, as if he'd been meant to stay that long-ago day in 1977 when he came knocking at the door in flip-flops. Now that he was back, her door was open to them (as long as he promised never to wear flip-flops again), and the trio was one loud, happy family, cooking up a storm. Skip loved chowing down Mom's big fiery Korean meals and listening to her talk about her childhood in Sinuiju and the mother she left behind while Ginger baked his dessert du jour. Mom seemed energized by having them close; she applied for U.S. citizenship, and on the very day she was sworn in as a proud American, she gave up her beloved Virginia Slims.

Lulu cocked her head, still sizing up the situation. *Skip and Ginger? Really?* "Skip and Francie seem closer in age and they both have that bad-ass look in their eye, you know?"

Ginger could only chuckle. How many times had she heard variations on that theme?

"So, Francie," Lulu wondered, "who's *your* guy?"

"No one special."

After nearly three years together, Francie had broken things off with Darren—despite his promise, he was drinking more than ever. Then, like a love junkie, she began seeing him again, a night here, a night there.

"Ma'am," Skip addressed Lulu, "how many Dark Break-Ups would you like today?"

While Skip finished up his sale, Ginger pulled Francie into the back room. Something was up.

"Everything okay?"

"Well . . ."

"What is it?"

Francie hesitated.

"Francie?"

"Darren's cheating on me," Francie blurted.

Ginger murmured, not completely surprised. "Why do you think he's cheating on you?"

"I spent the night at his place last night, and after he left for work this morning, his phone rang but I didn't pick up. The next thing I knew, a woman's voice was leaving a message for him."

"Oh, God. What did she say?"

"She was crying, actually, asking him why he never showed up at her house last night."

Ginger hugged her sister. "Let's face it, Francie, Darren's got too much baggage for a real relationship."

"Not only that, there's something I never told you."

"What?"

"I don't know if I can say it."

"Say it!"

"Darren can't tell the difference between our chocolate and the stuff from Peoples Drug store."

Ginger gasped. "Scumbag!"

When love bailed, a chocolate orgy was in order. Ginger tore the lid off a big box of prize-winning Naron chocolate because sometimes you just had to experience the ultimate in gluttony and dive into endless rows of button milk and dark chocolates, some

round, some square, some smooth, some swirly-topped, all glistening and warmed to room temperature.

"Who needs men?" Ginger indulged. "This is better than sex."

Francie groaned with pleasure. "Oh, my . . ."

When the chocolate orgy was over, so were Francie and Darren.
There were pleading phone messages, unanswered knocks at her
door, and cards in her mailbox.

Francie showed Ginger an accordion-style card with cartoon
renderings of one frog meeting another frog. "*If I never met you,*"
she read aloud, "*I never would have known you. And had I never
known you, I never would have loved you. But I met you and knew
you and loved you—and now I miss you, Face.*" Her sigh was heavy.
"Why couldn't he have just been faithful?"

Ginger shrugged. "Then he wouldn't have been Darren."

When Francie left Darren, "Dark Break-Up" took on a double
meaning: She went Greta Garbo. With men no longer in her field
of vision, all she did was write at home in her new apartment—
small but urbane, with wall-to-wall views of the Potomac—visit
Mom, and work at the shop. Indeed, there was no place she'd rather
be than at Chocolate Chocolate. Here, sadness took a holiday. For
hours at a time, she could forget about Darren. The revolving door
of customers was a godsend. She looked forward to her moments in
the Chat Corner with Gypsy Bess in a place where everything
would be okay, someday. Even watching her friend work herself
into a tizzy over the plight of the homeless—"The poor gal had two
little ones, one hanging off each hip!"—made Francie feel alive.
Even Dr. Zhivago, though ever silent, had a strength about him as
if he'd survived a hundred Siberian winters, a strength that made
Francie wish he would say something, anything, because surely,
like the candy bar in his hand, it would hold something good and
worth keeping, maybe even magical. And then there were new

customers like that big bear of a guy who always wore a fedora hat. Every day after lunch he would tip it or toss it while trying to decide between Dark Almond Bark and Dark Nonpareils. His wide-open friendly face made her smile.

Oh, and don't forget about the chocolate. A smooth gush of chocolate, any chocolate, was Francie's elixir.

Despite a decade of Valentine's Days under our belt, we could never really prepare for the level of energy it took to get through it, and the exhaustion afterward. Mom, however, seemed to know no bounds—throwing out that last carton of Virginia Slims gave her a new lease on life. These days she spent her mornings walking and half jogging around her neighborhood like she owned it.

"I come in and work today," she declared in the kitchen, running in place in her new Nikes.

"Are you serious?" Ginger questioned her.

"Soo," as Skip called her, short for Heisook, "you do know it's Valentine's Day, right?"

"I know," she shouted, still running, "and you need my help!"

We always would.

In the car on the way over to pick up Francie, Mom brought up a sore subject: "Francie not have Valentine again this year?"

Skip shook his head sadly. "I never thought I'd see the day when Francie would become a nun."

Mom sighed. "It been over year now. Something wrong with that girl?"

"Nothing's wrong," Ginger defended her, "she just needs some time and space."

At the close of business, the four of us decided to drive over to the southwest waterfront to celebrate Valentine's Day at Phillips

Seafood. In a half-moon booth with the day's cash receipts in a burlap sack squished between us, our quartet feasted on huge platters of shrimp, lobster, and clams, except for Francie who had ordered a veggie pasta. When Francie gave up men, she went whole hog and gave up *all* animals. As usual we found ourselves talking about all the characters who stood out that day.

"They really trampled him good, didn't they?" Skip said about the self-important talk show host who always thought he was above waiting in line.

"Happy Valentine's Day!" we all toasted, woozy on wine.

Zonked, we left the restaurant and headed toward the car two blocks away.

"You leave good tip?" Mom asked Skip.

His Popeye walk with a smile and a toot meant yes.

"He never leave me anything but dirty dish," she said playfully.

"I was feeling generous tonight, Soo."

"He always leave too much," she joked.

"Yeah, well it's not like I left the whole . . ." Suddenly Skip stopped dead in his tracks.

"What? What?" We crowded around him. "What's wrong?"

His face went pale. "Please tell me one of you has the sack of money."

"NO!!!!!!!!!!!!!!!"

Skip ran like the devil back to the restaurant. Paralyzed, we waited for him.

"You think money still there?" Mom fretted, then began mumbling in Korean. Her Yamagada cards were good today, but that was twelve hours ago.

"Hope so," we kept repeating, on the lookout for Skip.

Where was he, where was he?

"There he is!" We jumped. "And he's got the sack!"

"Whew," he said, out of breath, "it was still in the booth, right where we left it. Man, can you imagine getting *that* tip?"

Even on casual friday, the Bear wore his trademark hat, which he tipped our way.

"Hi folks, just got back." He grinned.

"Hi, there," we greeted him. Hard as we tried, we had so many ongoing conversations with so many customers that it was hard to keep track of who was going where and doing what, especially when we were still in acquaintance stage.

"You went to . . . ?" Ginger asked, waiting for him to fill in the blank.

He looked surprised, almost hurt, that we forgot. "Ireland."

"That's right," Ginger nodded.

"You said," Francie recalled, "you'd never been."

Skip, looking for a cherry cordial that had rolled on the ground, bellowed from below. "Did you have a good time?"

The Bear chuckled. "Oh, hi, I thought I heard you down there. Yes, Linda and I loved Ireland. So many little bookstores, and pubs on every corner. The people are so friendly. You know, we could use some village life in this country."

He seemed on the verge of saying more and our antennas went up: Maybe he wanted to get to know us a little better. We introduced ourselves, even Skip, or at least the backside of him.

"I'm Norman," he said. "Nice to meet all of you."

"So, Norman, are you in a Dark Almond Bark or Nonpareil mood today?" Francie found it easier to remember a customer's favorite chocolates than his or her name.

Pleased she remembered, the Bear said, "Well, the Dark Almond Bark's a better bang for your buck."

"Really? How so?"

"They're the same price per pound," Skip pointed out, still cherry cordial hunting.

"True," the Bear replied, "but with the Nonpareils, the little white candy dots fall off and into the bag. You don't eat them but you still pay for them. I could give you more exact calculations if you like."

Ginger laughed. "What do you do for a living, Norman?"

"I'm an actuary."

"Figures."

Before the Bear left, he took something from his pocket and handed it to us. "I couldn't resist picking this up from a little candy shop in Ireland."

A green box with a clear window encased a lovely milk chocolate shamrock the size of a heart. We'd been the recipients of token gifts from customers before, but this one, a lucky charm out of the blue, felt wonderfully personal. Affirming. It passed through each of our hands before we set it up on a shelf and pronounced: "And there's where it'll stay."

Just as the Bear left, Skip stood up. Ginger scoffed at her husband. "You gotta be more conversational with customers, Skip. Get to know them face-to-face. One way or another, you're always finding excuses to hide."

"Sorry but I'm just not customer oriented. Like you and Francie always say, I'm a behind-the-scenes kind of guy."

Ginger relented. "Then at least smile once in a while, for God's sake!"

"Ginge," Francie issued out of the corner of her mouth, "he *is* smiling, remember?"

"Oh, right."

Still, side by side, we crossed our arms.

"Skip, was there really a cherry cordial on the ground?" Francie asked him, point-blank.

"Yes and quit ganging up on me!"

"Well, where is it?" Ginger hmmphed. "I don't see it anywhere."

"I ate it. Five-second rule."

Down the road we got to know the Bear a little better every day. Skip soon learned that the Bear, like himself, was a sailing man, so they planned a day of glorious cruising on Chesapeake Bay. His wife, Linda, was the manager of the Borders bookstore in White Flint Mall, and she invited us to give a chocolate talk to their customers one Thursday evening. Stella passed around free samples of chocolate creams and cherries donated by Naron, and a grand time was had by all. Afterward, the whole gang, including Mom, dined at a nearby Buddhist restaurant where the servers poured water from ancient-looking jugs.

"Cheers," Stella said. "In case anyone cares, my feet hurt like hell."

Over time, Francie's spirits began to lift. Still, for the most part, she remained reclusive. After a day at Chocolate Chocolate, closing the door behind her and writing into the wee hours was all she knew now. Sometimes she would answer the phone and hear Gypsy Bess's voice on the other end, checking up on her. Always evening, when her floppy hat was hung up for the day.

"I met a nice young doctor in my doctor's building on 18th Street the other day and I told him all about you."

Francie joked, "Why, is he a shrink?"

"No, he's single and good-lookin' and said maybe he'd stop by your shop sometime. Would you like to hear more?"

"I'd rather hear about you, Bess."

Gypsy Bess's zest for life awed her: The sixty-something was as energetic as any thirty-something, playing tennis, volunteering at the Children's Museum in northeast D.C., helping a friend with his new beer-brewing venture. Yet what intrigued Francie more were Gypsy Bess's stories about growing up during the Depression without a mother, her juicy remembrances of taking a bus with her girlfriends to spend a day in New York City during World War II in the hopes of meeting handsome GIs on furlough at dances in hotels. Firsthand American history with hearty detail. You couldn't find that in any book, and Francie was so hungry to hear more she could stay on the phone all night with her friend, but sooner or later, even Gypsy Bess would grow hoarse and it was time to say good night.

Francie was finally confident enough to share her writings with Gypsy Bess, who ate them up like her Chocolate-Dipped Apricots, one by one.

"Here's a new one, Bess," Francie said one afternoon in the shop. "The ink hasn't even dried yet."

Gypsy Bess skimmed the first page before stashing it in her handbag for late-night reading. "The main character in this one sounds suspiciously like someone we all knew and tried to love. Someone like . . . Darren, perhaps?"

Ginger stole a Monster Mint Patty from the middle candy case, smiling. "Gee, I wonder why."

Francie took the liberty of breaking off a big chunk of her sister's midday treat. A bit of white cream started to escape but she caught it in the nick of time. "Sometimes it's good to get stuff off your chest and still call it fiction," she said, mouth full.

"Well, darlin'"—Gypsy Bess looked up as her reading glasses

slid down her pretty nose—"if you ever write about me, don't forget all the hugs and lovin' words I gave you, okay?"

"I'll never forget."

Sometimes Francie felt as if the bite-sized chocolates stashed all over her apartment in crumpled-up bags, warm and fragrant from being under a sofa pillow or pile of papers, were all that sustained her. Unravel, open . . . the potpourri of chocolate malted balls, almonds, and raisins made her feel like she actually might survive this dark chapter of her life that went deeper than a broken heart. All her bad choices and self-doubts, the rejection letters for stories too personal to talk about in the light of day, were nearly killing her. Only chocolate, everything wrapped up in it, and her writing dream kept her going.

Then, one day, Francie got a letter in the mail from a magazine that made her hands tremble so badly she could hardly read it. She was used to getting the white and cream-colored envelopes, the smartly typewritten return addresses. Her heart didn't miss a beat as she tore them open, one after another, knowing what to expect. But this time was different: Her first short story was accepted for publication. Its circulation was barely a thousand, but so what? Someone thought her work was good enough to publish.

A few months later when the magazine came out, she saw her name in print and broke down. All her nights alone and wondering had been worth it. They meant something. Mom took the gang out for a celebratory dim sum brunch at Fortune in Falls Church.

"Wish your daddy here," Mom said.

We all agreed, clinking teacups.

"So, Francie, what's the story called?" Skip asked, pouring everyone another round.

She hesitated. "'Someday Today Will Seem Like a Long Time Ago.'"

"That's a very true statement, but what's the title of your story?"

"That *is* the title."

"Oh! So what's it about?"

"Heartbreak."

Once Francie's first work was accepted for publication, boom, boom, boom, doors seemed to open. By the mid-'90s, her fiction had appeared in a dozen magazines, and now she and Ginger were toying with the possibility of a collaborative effort writing for kids. The year before, Ginger had finally penned and polished "The Milk Boy," a picture book manuscript about a boy "who rose when the moon was still in the sky . . . Afterward, on a rusty old bicycle, he made his round of milk deliveries to wealthy Japanese families in Seoul . . ." Holding her breath, she sent it off to a half-dozen children's publishing houses, only to see each one returned with the same sentiment:

We love this little portrait of an impoverished Korean child who daydreams of a better life while he rides his bicycle. However, we're looking for a story with movement, one that tells a complete story. If you decide to draw out this vignette, we'd love to see it again. In any event, please send any future works our way.

Each time, Ginger sighed. "I still don't get it."

"Ugh, they're the rules and regulations of storytelling, Ginge," Francie kept explaining, having heard it all before. "They want your milk boy to travel from Point A to Point B to Point C, not pedal in place, so to speak."

Ginger protested. "But I *like* him just pedaling and dreaming. That *is* the story. And I'm *not* changing a word."

Although "The Milk Boy" wasn't the story Ginger was meant to share with the world, one sleepless midnight, lightning struck.

Ecstatic, she picked up the phone.

"Wake up, Francie!"

Blinded by the hour and a just-switched-on lamp, Francie couldn't see a thing. "Is it Mom?"

A couple of years earlier, a commercial truck had run a red light and hit Mom's car on one of those rare occasions when she was driving, leaving her with a torn rotator cuff. Our old rock-and-roll lawyer George represented her on a contingency basis and won her a small settlement. Despite her full recovery, we were still shaken up.

"Yes, it's Mom," Ginger spoke, "but not what you're thinking. I just came up with a great idea for a children's book!"

"Can't it wait till morning?"

"No."

"Hold on." Francie paused, waiting for her eyes to focus and her heart to stop pounding. "Okay, shoot."

"I think we should write about Mom's escape from North Korea when she was a child. We could put ourselves in her shoes, step by step, as she made her dangerous journey. Talk about going from Point A to Point B to Point C. And I even have a title: 'My Freedom Trip.' What do you think?" Ginger asked.

How many times had we heard about Mom's dangerous journey across the mountains?

"I think it's a great idea, too, Ginge. But . . ."

"But what?"

"Well, you sure you don't want to write it alone? It's your idea."

"We're her daughters." Ginger was feverishly convinced. "We were meant to write it together."

"When you put it that way . . ."

"Yes, and it'll be like chocolate."

"How so?"

"An experience beyond words."

Re-created, at least Mom's lifetime of sorrow wouldn't go to waste. And it would be a tribute to Mom, and her mom, from us, as daughters and granddaughters. Closure, perhaps.

Chapter 14

Our House Truffle

A secret recipe

After our years of typing out entertaining sketches about our customers, coauthoring a real book seemed like a natural next step. As Ginger had predicted, the experience of writing together was joyous if not emotional, especially considering that *My Freedom Trip: A Child's Escape from North Korea* so closely mimicked our mother's actual experience. To our delight, publishers leaped with offers—maybe our chocolate shamrock really *was* our lucky charm. One condition: Nearly every publisher begged us to change the ending of the story to a happy one for children, so that mother and daughter were reunited in the end. But like Korea's permanent split, the two remained divided and never saw each other again. Why sugarcoat the truth?

"This no fairy tale," was Mom's reaction, and we agreed.

Only one publisher shared our vision, and that was the one we chose to publish Mom's story. It was 1997; our book was due out the following year. We couldn't wait.

Not all was blissful: A series of daily bomb threats phoned in to the management office of our building during lunchtime was killing our business. This went on for months, all spring, and today was no exception.

Ginger sighed. "We have to close up shop again."

Like everyone else in Oz, we had no choice but to roam around the block like orphans and wait for the security guards to take down the yellow tape, the signal we could go back in. As we locked up, we saw Edgar outside, stooped over our window displays. For many years now, Edgar and his fanciful bow ties had been a fixture downtown, in our lives and psyches. What began with a Christmas list developed into a fascination for chocolate collectibles.

"Hi, Francie, hi, Ginger! I'm just admiring your chocolate butterflies in the window."

Big as monarchs, our butterflies were whimsical replicas of the real thing. With bittersweet bases, the tops were hand-painted with white chocolate tinted purple, yellow, and pink in swirl, stripe, and dot designs. Like real butterflies and bow ties, they were eye-catching.

"Are these new?" Edgar inquired. "I don't believe I've ever noticed them before."

"We get them in every spring and summer," Ginger informed him, "along with the chocolate starfish and ladybugs and seashells."

"But the butterflies are special," Francie confided.

Once Dad was gone, so were his gardens. Only the bamboo survived. Actually, without proper maintenance, Mom soon had a jungle on her hands. Many times we went out with Mom to battle the bamboo, but the harder we yanked out their roots, the faster they shot back up. Only pandas could clear up this mess, we would grumble to one another.

Seven years passed. Seven flowerless springs. Seven springs of bamboo gone wild. Mom spent one afternoon hunched over in agony as she pulled and yanked, tied twine around cut stalks, then dragged the bundles to the curb for trash pickup. A thankless task, sweat running down her neck, not how a once-privileged girl with servants at her beck and call would imagine spending her days. In a moment of self-pity, a delicate purple monarch butterfly appeared in the bamboo mist. More stoic than her daughters, she was somehow touched.

"Hello, butterfly," she softly sang.

Every woman who has weathered war or widowhood knows this song. The song of tragedy.

The creature fluttered, it danced, it serenaded her—its wings were talking to her. And didn't leave her side all afternoon. Wouldn't. She could have sworn it was following her. In the way she believed in the prophecy of her Yamagada cards, this was mystical.

"I know who you are, butterfly . . ."

That spring, seven years after Dad passed away, the rose trellis on the side of her house miraculously bloomed.

"My, what a lovely story," Edgar murmured. "I'll be back to buy some butterflies for my nieces." Before he went on his way, he congratulated us. "Skip told me you sold your book. I can say I knew you when."

Waiting out the bomb scare and wandering around our neighborhood, recently designated the Golden Triangle by the government, we passed customers left and right.

There was Dan, a handsome, upbeat guy who stopped by every week or two for a sizable gummy bear fix. We called him Dashing Dan for the striking figure he cut in his Armani suits and the way he dashed in and out of our store. He rarely waited around for his change, be it ten cents or ten dollars.

"Hi, ladies," he said.

"How's it going?" we asked.

"Great," he replied without stopping. Even outside, he had one foot out the door.

That said, whenever Dashing Dan was scooping out gummy bears, he would reiterate that if we ever had real estate concerns, he'd be happy to help us out. He was president of a company that built and leased real estate, and his family owned many properties in town including the building across the street. We assumed that if his partners were anything like him, they bore little resemblance to our Landlord, who seemed to have a bad habit of kicking tenants out of the building on a regular basis. Still, as long as the Landlord's people stayed out of our hair, we stopped short of calling them the Evil Empire.

Dashing Dan was halfway down the street when we thought to call after him. "How's your gummy bear stash?"

"Getting low! I'll be in to restock later this week!"

Inevitably, we bumped into Bill-About-Town on the corner of Connecticut and K. His appearance on the *Rosie O'Donnell Show* last year for a humorous book he wrote about how to outwit squirrels only sparked more book projects—he seemed to be writing ten books in the time it took him to stroke his red beard.

Amused, we said, "Is there anything you *don't* do?"

"What can I say, guys, I wear many hats." He smiled, straightening the collar of his Aerosmith T-shirt. "Hey," he got quizzical, "why aren't you in the shop?"

"Another bomb threat," we croaked.

"That's *still* going on? You poor guys. And poor me! My family won't let me back in the house today without a weekend's worth of Chocolate-Covered Pretzels, so I'll be back downtown before you guys close," he promised.

After much aimless walking, we sat down at a popular people-watching spot at the edge of the circular water fountain across the street from our shop. At any given moment, we could each whip out a dog-eared manuscript from our handbag, but who was in the mood? We were tired, not inspired. Spotting a familiar little figure pulling on our doors to no avail, Ginger perked up.

"What's Stella doing here?"

"We're supposed to do our Christmas orders today," Francie said, flagging her down. "Over here!"

Stella seemed to take a lifetime crossing the street in her ill-fitting pumps, cursing the windy day for mussing her hair.

"Not another bomb threat?"

We grimaced. "Can you believe it?"

"What a bitch."

"Exactly."

"No, I mean this girdle! I'm not like you girls who can just plop yourselves down anywhere you please. Oh, my God," she moaned as she lowered herself in slow motion. Once seated, she tsked. "It's so goddamned hot today."

"So take off your sweater," Francie suggested.

"What, show arms? I'm not a slut, dear. Speaking of sluts, listen, girls, before we get down to work, I have an announcement to make: That buffoon I called a husband for thirty-six years left me for another woman. His high school sweetheart, of all things."

As close as we were, Stella had always been somewhat tight-lipped about her husband. We knew more about her first husband, the love of her life who fell ill with Hodgkin's disease shortly after their honeymoon and suffered through painful medical experiments before dying. This one was a grump, we knew firsthand from our single encounter with him years ago, when he stopped at our shop to drop off a few cases of chocolates for her. Resentfully, he threw the boxes down without a word, not even a greeting. Now we corralled around our old friend.

"Are you okay, Stella?"

"I'm selling the house and moving to Leisure World, I'm fine," she fibbed. "I don't do gushy scenes. I just want my favorite two gals"—her voice broke—"to know what happened."

Stella handed us Christmas flyers that whipped in the wind as she got out her order pad. All the while we were exchanging helpless looks: What to do? What to say? She was as near and dear to us as a human being could be, but her Little General armor was hard to penetrate.

"Come on, girls, hurry up and tell me what you'd like." She tried to giddyup through our pity as the first of two tears fell on our order sheet. "Shit."

"Perfect description of him," Ginger remarked.

"We didn't have a storybook marriage and he was a royal pain in the ass, but he was *my* pain in the ass," Stella said, "and when you're married as long as we were, and you've been together through thick and thin and three kids, you don't walk out, for God's sake. But he did, and all I can say is, *I'm* the better person."

"Better-looking, too," Francie said with a loving pat.

The compliment made her smile, reclaim some of her spunk. "Screw work—Christmas orders can wait. Who feels like getting a drink?"

Across the street, the yellow tape wasn't coming down anytime soon. We hopped down.

"By the way," Stella glanced around, "where's Skip?"

Sometimes we thought Skip was secretly glad whenever there was a bomb threat because it gave him an excuse to go outside. He got antsy working behind the counter, claustrophobic, even. Or maybe he just wanted to be free of us.

"You two are nicer to customers than you are to me," he complained the next morning. "I swear, sometimes you're the Twisted Sisters."

Francie, checking out her hair in the mirror above the cash register, just laughed. "Oh, bullshit, Skip."

"Bullshit, nuttin'."

"Listen," Ginger had argued, "we'd be nicer to you if you just stayed in one spot!"

Impossible. Whenever we got the green light to open back up for business, Skip was nowhere to be found. We reopened for business to a flood of chocoholics, as usual sans Skip. Things got crazy! For twenty minutes it was Valentine's Day in May. Tissue, tongs, turtles flying everywhere! After saying good-bye to the last customer, we took a deep breath.

Just as we recovered, Skip meandered in. One look around at the empty shop made him sigh like Eeyore.

"No customers, eh?"

Ginger was fuming. "Where were you?"

"I was over on Pennsylvania Avenue checking out Belgique. They were packed with customers!"

Belgique was the new chocolate operation in town; in a year's time, they'd opened up shops all over the metropolitan area, claiming they air-freighted their Belgian chocolates daily—no truth in advertising there; if they did, their bonbons would go for a thousand dollars a pound. We snarled at the mere mention of them, as on several occasions Belgique workers stood outside our shop handing out gold coins trying to steal our customers. Each gold coin could be redeemed for five dollars' worth of free chocolate.

"Well, we were packed too, Skip, and lost sales because you were too busy spying on them," she retorted.

"They're gonna run us out of business."

"Hah! Over my dead body," Francie said. "Look, Skip, just love *our* business and stop thinking about the competition. They'll probably be gone before you know it."

Through a drooping mustache, Skip mumbled something to the contrary.

Later that week, he was out and about again, long after the security guards had taken down the yellow tape. Ginger was more incensed than ever.

"If he's spying on Belgique again, two things are going to happen. First, I'm going to rip off his 'stache. Then I'll staple it to his forehead."

Just then Skip stumbled in with a fatal pronouncement: "Our lives are over."

"Again?" Ginger smirked.

"I'm not kidding this time. You're never going to believe what I just found out."

Wearily, Francie crossed her arms. Sometimes his Mr. Doom and Gloom act was funny. Sometimes it wasn't. "What?"

"I was on my way to Borders when I noticed a lady at the corner. She was holding a clipboard and a map, looking dazed."

"So?" we said.

"I asked her if I could point her in the right direction, and she said she was looking for a particular space. She told me the address and guess what?"

"What?"

"It turned out to be one of the empty spaces in our building."

Ginger was ready to pull her hair out. "Get to the point, Skip."

"The point is, she's planning to open a Candy Circus franchise in that space *just a few doors down from us.* The Landlord offered her a lease—I saw it with my own two eyes."

We were speechless. White hot with rage. Damn it, they *were* the Evil Empire!

Our distress must've empowered Skip, because the next thing we knew he was thumbing through our Rolodex, mustache trembling, ready to blow. "Don't you worry, I'll handle this."

In a matter of moments, Skip was berating the present-day leasing agent.

"Your mother-*#/@! gig is up!"

Our jaws dropped, as he wasn't one for profanity.

He went on, nearly growling. "According to our lease, and I have it right in front of me, man, you're not supposed to lease out space to another confectionary."

His next threat, to sue them, had us euphoric. We high-fived in the background. Skip was more than just a handyman!

The leasing guy indicated that Candy Circus sold more candy, per se, than chocolate, so technically it wasn't competitive with our operation. A fine legal line, but Skip blew it off.

"Technically, that's bullshit, mother-*#/@!"

After slamming down the phone, without so much as a good-bye, Skip let out a sigh.

"So?" we asked him.

Skip was a Cheshire Cat—all grins. "He was like Elvis; all shook up!"

In the end, the Evil Empire agreed not to lease out the space to Candy Circus on several conditions: We renew our lease immediately, agree to fix everything on a construction punch list, and commit to staying there for another ten years. As it was, we had already renewed our lease in 1993 and weren't due to renew for another few years. But we had no qualms about renewing now. As far as we were concerned, even if our energies these days were divided between the shop and our writing, we'd keep Chocolate Chocolate going until our last breath. How could one live without chocolate? But before we signed on the dotted line, we demanded a look at the punch list.

It was looooong.

"Piece of cake," Skip said. "I was planning to give this store a total face-lift anyway. Let's face it, it's looking as worn-out as the rest of us."

Francie coughed. "Speak for yourself."

"Skip, you're the only worn-out-looking one here," Ginger said in jest. "All those worry wrinkles and—"

"What? What?"

"I see a couple of grays in your 'stache."

Skip ran to the mirror in panic. "Oh, my God, you're right. When did I turn into an old man?"

Surely our youth had faded, but despite what the calendar said, we didn't feel appreciably older than the day we opened for business thirteen years earlier, shivering in our coats. Though Edgar's Christmas list had shrunk to twelve pages, and indeed many of our customers had retired and moved on or were grandparents now, we would forever see ourselves in a certain light, in a place where time stood still.

Not that life hadn't changed. Ginger and Skip, who seemed like they'd known each other their whole lives, were trying to have a baby but it just wasn't happening, much to Skip's chagrin. Francie, coming out of her Greta Garbo spell, had her focus on a different kind of baby; she was putting the finishing touches on a little book, a novella about a baker's quest to make the perfect cake. Maybe Francie couldn't boil an egg, but her infatuation with characters who could often found their way into her fiction. And soon enough, a small literary press accepted her book for publication.

The shop closed for renovations while Skip went right down the list, serving as both contractor and subcontractor, painting, repairing, even supervising the replacement of our eyesore floors with black granite that gleamed like a moonlit lake. Though it still ran behind the counter and back room, the crack out front was gone. Forever?

"Nah," Skip said, already hearing the sound of it coming back. *Crack.*

Skip was in the right place at the right time: The Candy Circus deal was scrapped and he'd serendipitously saved our day. Now Skip had earned the right to spend an hour in the new Starbucks down the street, talk to Jamal about the plight of D.C. government, and come back with cold coffee. We no longer felt quite so entitled to nag him about his disappearing act.

To top off our relief, Belgique abruptly went out of business. We celebrated by breaking up a large tray of Cashew Bark into bite-sized pieces, offering samples while they lasted. Most reached happily for the tray, but Dr. Zhivago, always looking like he just walked out of a Tolstoy novel, demurred without a word. We had become so accustomed to his silent presence that we held back a verbal greeting and nodded to him almost instinctively. Skip was in a boisterous mood and was bustling between the front and back room reminding us that we were here to stay for a while.

Amid our impromptu Cashew Bark party, he had an idea. "We need something we can call our own," he called from his desk in back. "A House Truffle."

Ginger frowned, hoping a certain someone didn't hear that. Alas . . .

"That's it." Francie air-clapped. "A House Truffle! What a great idea."

"No, it's not a great idea. Skip's just frustrated because we can't make a baby," Ginger explained. "So he wants to make truffles."

"Whatever the reason, Ginge, it's the truth. We do need something we can call our own, and you're the one who can make it happen." When the phone began ringing, Francie went to get it. "And I'm telling you, it'll be the best truffle on earth."

"I don't know . . . ," Ginger uttered, feeling cornered.

Skip emerged from the back room, dismayed. "I just checked our records, and last year we sold over forty thousand Candy Jar truffles," he reported.

"So?" she said.

"Maria's a sweet little old lady who makes all those truffles herself. Why can't we do that?" he demanded. "Why can't we have our own House Truffle? An offering from our own blood, sweat, and tears."

"For all kinds of reasons," Ginger said while cleaning shelves with a pink feather duster. "Maria's got two daughters helping her and a whole factory. And we've got books to write. Francie's on a new novel, I'm thinking about one, and we're halfway through a new children's book. Unless we're helping customers, do you ever see us without a manuscript in our hands? Plus, I don't know the first thing about making truffles."

Skip rubbed his hands together. Once he got something in his head, there was no letting it go. "I'll help. Even better, Francie and I'll be your little Willie Wonka helpers."

Francie got off the phone, laughing. "That was Kahlua Lady. She's sending her husband in to pick up her order instead of Chauffeur Geoffrey. He'll be identifying himself as 'Mr. Kahlua Lady.'"

"Don't you see?" Skip kept badgering Ginger. "Kahlua Lady would buy *your* truffles, if you made them. Willy Wonka, Willy Wonka . . ." he chanted as if to hypnotize her into a chocolate trance.

Ginger tried to picture Skip and Francie in an assembly line. Talk about a recipe for disaster. They had no idea what an undertaking this would be, or exactly *whose* blood, sweat, and tears were at stake. And neither would be as helpful as little Mike at the food cart, no way.

"You'll just get in the way and Francie's hair will get into everything," she predicted.

"Come on," Skip begged, "it'll be a piece of cake."

"Will you stop saying that? You've never even *made* a cake!"

Why argue? Skip was halfway out the door.

"Where are you going?" she asked.

"To Borders to buy some books on truffle making. If we start experimenting now, we'll be selling them by Christmas."

Waving her feather duster, Ginger yelled after him, "Are you nuts? Christmas is right around the corner!"

But so was Skip already.

"Any excuse for another escape." She sighed.

Dr. Zhivago looked up from the candy bar rack, as if her sigh had awoken him from a long winter nap.

"How are you?" he greeted us.

After a decade of silence, we were stunned. No Russian accent. Midwestern, maybe.

"Hi," we both said.

Dr. Zhivago returned to the candy bars, when suddenly he turned to us with a faraway twinkle in his eye.

"I couldn't help but eavesdrop on your conversation. Truffles, eh? You know, when my father was a young man in Russia after World War I, food and jobs were scarce. But he was one of the lucky ones; he got a job in a chocolate factory where his duty was to clean the chocolate vats. Every night. His pay was all the chocolate he could scrape off and eat from the vats. I guess that the novelty wore off in the worst way—for over fifty years, my father couldn't stand the sight, the smell, even the thought of chocolate!" He shook his head sadly. "I always tried to give him some of mine—I always had a sweet tooth. But he refused, every time. I never gave up, though, it actually became a little game." His face creased into a smile, remembering. "Chocolate? Not for me, he'd always say . . . But then out of the blue, after the usual prodding from me, he agreed to a taste, just a bite of my dark candy bar."

"And . . . ?"

Dr. Zhivago looked serious. "At that moment, the love of chocolate came back to him."

Dr. Zhivago's faced flushed with nostalgia, and we, having recovered from his distinct Wisconsin farm accent, imagined the delighted expression of an elderly European man as the chocolate slid down his throat for the first time in half a century.

We were quiet a moment.

"What a lovely story," Francie told him. "And after that?"

Dr. Zhivago smiled; no matter how old he was today, he would always be a proud son. "My father accepted chocolate from me for the rest of his life."

〜

Ginger took Dr. Zhivago's surprise story as a sign. Like diving into a vat of chocolate, Ginger spent the next week reading all about the science of chocolate as well as the art of truffle making, and before Sunday, her kitchen had turned into a chocolate factory.

"Told you this would be a blast," Skip said, cracking open a beer and watching a Redskins game.

"Where's the thermometer?"

"Hold on, I'll get it for you in a sec. I just want to see the kickoff."

"No, right now, Skip," Ginger said, already steamed enough to melt every chocolate chunk on the kitchen counter. "Francie, can you wash the wooden spoon for me?"

"Can it wait five minutes, Ginge? I just did my nails."

"Willie Wonka, my foot," she grumbled, wishing for a little helper like the one we used to see at his parents' food cart. *"Where's Mike?"*

Mom cut short a Yamagada game and came running over. "I do for you, Ginger," she said, turning on the water.

"Thanks, Mom," she said. "Those clowns are worthless in the kitchen."

Without question, Callebaut, the Belgian block chocolate, would serve as the couverture, the outer truffle shell that had a higher cocoa butter content than regular chocolate for an extra-glossy finish. It was the standard coating for all premium truffles. But not all truffle centers were created equal, and Ginger's hope was to create the ultimate ball of joy—the ganache center. Channeling the wunderkind mastermind of her Easy-Bake Oven days, Ginger broke chocolate, melted chocolate, and stirred chocolate into cream, butter, crème de cacao, and fresh vanilla bean, blending different brands: Lindt with Guittard, Perugina with Ghirardelli; Neuhaus with Valrhona, for starters. This became a full-time project, and now she stayed home during the week with Mom serving as her helper and guinea pig. Since Mom had given up her Virginia Slims, her taste buds had come alive and well—she could identify most combos spot-on.

"I taste everything now!"

Good thing because all this chocolate in Ginger's hair, nose, and mouth was making her queasy. She thought this day would never come. Still, she took little nibbles until one turned out just the way she imagined her perfect truffle would look, taste, and feel on her tongue. One Sunday morning in August when Skip was downtown on his hands and knees with putty and caulk—yes, the crack was back—she called and told him to come home *now*. Then she phoned Francie.

"Can you come over right away?"

"Everything okay?"

"Yup, just hurry over."

Francie dropped her pen and put down her manuscript. Very little these days could pull her away from her writing, especially on her day off, but the urgency in Ginger's voice meant something was up.

A half hour later the whole clan was gathered in Mom's kitchen.

"I have two announcements to make," Ginger said, flushed with excitement.

"First, my House Truffle is ready to make its debut. It passed my test and Mom's test. Now it's Francie's turn."

Like a cake fresh from the Easy-Bake Oven, she presented her sister with a single truffle on a dessert plate.

"It's so perfect, Ginge." She paused.

"What are you waiting for?"

It looked like a true truffle plucked from the ground, deep and dark and dusted with cocoa powder. Francie held it up to the light, then took a little velvety bite that proved volcanic.

"Three words come to mind: chocolat de vie." She couldn't believe that Ginger had made this magical morsel. And she felt partly responsible for encouraging her in the first place.

Skip frowned. "Hey, where's mine? Don't I have a say in this? Don't forget, this was my idea."

"I've got something else for you," she said.

"Besides a truffle?"

"Yes."

Ginger brought his hands to her belly. "Your first child."

Mom closed her eyes in prayer. "My baby having baby. Your daddy would cry."

Chapter 15

Five Star Bar

Pillows of chocolate bliss

In that deliciously stolen hour after her monthly examination with Dr. Garreau, Ginger was in seventh heaven, traveling back to the shop full of good news. At four and a half months, she was fine; baby was fine. Deemed an "older" mom-to-be at thirty-four, Ginger had undergone an amniocentesis to confirm that a healthy fetus was growing in her belly. Test: A-plus. Feeling celebratory, she and Skip had stopped at the nearby Whole Foods for a brown bag gourmet lunch: juice, prepared paninis, and fresh fruit salad. Devouring it all in the car on the way to the shop was just what the doctor ordered.

"Listen," Skip said, steering with one hand, eating with the other, "it's time to put your House Truffles out for sale."

"Be quiet. I told you, I'm not ready."

"There's no time like the present. It's nearly November. Shoppers are getting ideas for Christmas. I don't get why you're so reluctant. Francie and I have already been spreading the word."

Ginger took a sip of juice and looked out the window. "For one thing, I'm pregnant and morning sickness is no walk in the park. Plus, I don't know if I have the energy to make Christmas truffles. And what if nobody likes them? You want me to miscarry?"

"Don't worry," Skip said, pulling into the garage, "even Eeyore says they're gonna be a hit."

Back in the shop, Francie was eager to know the upshot of Ginger's visit. "Everything cool at Dr. G's?" Francie said, feeling her sister's tummy behind the counter. "You sure there's a baby in there?"

Even after Ginger's ultrasound and an amniocentesis, Francie couldn't quite believe her little sister was pregnant. Not that Francie had a maternal bone in her body, but she was happy for her sister.

"Everything's cool," Ginger said, polishing off the last of her lunch—a pickle—with pleasurable crunch. "Except Skip had to bring up the House Truffles again. He wants me to make a batch to actually put out for sale *now*."

"I'm going to have to side with Skip, Ginge. It's time."

By December, Ginger was getting quite round; so big she had to give up tennis. She and Skip had become competitive players, but her racket would be collecting dust for a while. Since she couldn't do much of anything else, she was secretly happy to be making truffles. One morning she toted in a batch to the shop.

"I should probably debut my House Truffle today before Chubby Hubby eats them all," she joked, a bit jealous. The current literature claimed that chocolate was a no-no for pregnant women, the darker the more dangerous, as caffeine was the culprit—and make no mistake, these House Truffles were darkly dangerous. "You're sure they're good, Francie?"

"Please, they're awesome."

Ginger sighed. She was dreaming of the day she could bite into a House Truffle to see if it was just as she remembered. One bite would do. Haunted by cravings, Ginger's eyes lingered lovingly on her bittersweet favorites, especially the Fraises des Bois—strawberry cream, seeds and all, enrobed in chocolate. Hell, even the lowly Cashew Cluster she once dubbed a Plain Jane was looking pretty damn good right now. Stop, stop . . . For now, fond memories would have to do.

Christmas chocolates were in the air, packed in emerald and ruby boxes, tins, and baskets. Every year the shop glittered a bit more than the year before. Our newest guests to the party were Lake Champlain Chocolates from Vermont, a progressive, all-natural line of gourmet chocolates. Their chunky Five Star Bars were teeth-sinking buttery bliss, especially the Caramel Bar, a silken, not chewy, plump pillow of chocolate and caramel and almonds that would make any Scrooge smile. Also new were Joseph Schmidt Confections from San Francisco, a company with huge wow factor. Their hand-painted batik boxes not only caught every eye on the street, they were two gifts in one: chocolates plus a keepsake container for letters or small treasures. With Joseph Schmidt boxes around, Mom's oval making days were over. At sixty-eight, her dewy skin was deceiving—to us, she was forever fifty—but the fact was, she wasn't as steady with the glue gun as she used to be.

Between ringing up sales and chocolate chitchat, Ginger transferred her House Truffles to a large silver platter with a gloved hand. Despite their rustic appearance, they were too delicate for tongs.

"Voilà, world."

And there they sat like a pyramid of nuggets, on top of the counter for all to see. More than the gold shimmer from their cocoa-dusted loveliness, the dark chocolate perfume was intense, giving off the rich smell of the cocoa beans they came from.

Before Ginger could even finish writing the HOUSE TRUFFLE sign, a customer happened upon them.

"Are those new?" the gentleman asked Francie.

Setting down her calligraphy pen, Ginger fled to the back room and closed the door. But once there, she pressed her ear to the door. In her condition, rejection might be too much to bear. Fortunately, her critic gave them a swooning review and asked Francie to box up a dozen, please.

"Coming up."

This scenario repeated itself all morning as customers trickled in. Francie rang up a lot of House Truffles and Ginger spent a lot of time hiding in the back room.

Later that afternoon, a fashionable woman slinked up to the tray. Finger to her lips: "What are *those?*"

Francie spoke with supreme confidence. "Our House Truffles. Sample one. It's dark on dark."

"The only way to go," the customer sang, shedding her faux leopard gloves.

Once again, Ginger ran into the back room and pressed her ear to the door. She held her breath.

The woman took a taste and stepped back. "Pardon my French . . ."

"*Oui?*"

"But *mon Dieu*, these are downright pornographic."

"My sister made them."

"You can't be serious. Where is she? I'd love to meet the chef."

Glowing from the review, Ginger emerged. "Did you like them?" she asked, as if she didn't know.

"Like them? I *love* them!"

"Thank you!"

"No, thank *you*. I'd like to place an order, if I could."

Ginger's eyes danced. "Sure, I'd be happy to pack you up a box."

"Actually," the customer said, reaching in her handbag and whipping out a business card, "I need to place a large order."

Ooh, a large order! She could make them in her spare time, especially since her morning sickness was gone and Stella volunteered to help out during the holidays. Maybe Skip was right—our House Truffles might be a hit!

"I'm from a law firm and we're looking for client gifts. How much would a box cost?"

Francie stepped up with an empty black velvet box embossed with our silver logo. Striking. "This box would hold fifteen truffles and is priced at—"

"Does it come with a bow?"

"Of course. A crimson bow with silver string. See?"

"Fabulous. I'll take five hundred and thirty-five, please."

"Excuse me?" Francie coughed. "Five hundred and thirty-five . . . *truffles?*"

"No, five hundred and thirty-five *boxes.*"

Francie looked over at her truffle-making sis. How much manpower would it take . . . ?

"When do you need them?" Ginger asked cautiously.

"In about a week—is that doable?"

We rented space in a licensed commercial kitchen where, over the next seven days and nights, Ginger single-handedly rolled eight thousand and twenty-five House Truffle balls and lined them up like soldiers on sheets of wax paper before dipping each one into a warm, tempered vat of couverture. She didn't like this kitchen, it was cold and lifeless; it didn't have the warm hearth of her kitchen at home, the kitchen where we had cooked up a storm with the Easy-Bake Oven. Flour and batter everywhere!

Francie had tried to help with the rolling and dipping, but it was all a bit much for her. Cocoa powder flew in her contacts, which didn't help matters. Her truffle balls were all different shapes and sizes, some big, some small, some round, some oval.

"We're like Lucy and Ethel," she remarked.

"Yeah, without the laughs," Ginger snapped, in ill humor. "What happened to you in the kitchen? Back in our Easy-Bake Oven days, you were in charge and I was the little helper."

"Guess I lost my touch, Ginge. Besides, that was nearly thirty years ago!"

Ginger groaned. "Where's Mike?"

Francie's main job was to carefully fill our embossed black velvet boxes with House Truffles once they cooled and set, which happened in batches. The finishing touch was to ribbon the boxes up. In between those duties, she fetched Ginger tea, set out their usual panini lunch from Whole Foods, found good tunes on the portable radio, and go-go danced.

"Hey, Ginge, remember when I wanted to be a go-go dancer like the girls on *Shindig*?"

Not amused. "That was before my time."

For Ginger, so exhausted she could scream, there was no joy of cooking here. On the seventh night, when the last House Truffle was dipped and powdered, she tore off her apron and threw up her arms. Cocoa powder flew everywhere.

"I'm done—forever!"

Skip was gathering up bags full of boxes to carry to the car.

"Yeah, right, honey, your House Truffle will be so popular we'll be *living* in this kitchen."

We? Ginger ripped off his wire rims and yelled, "You're clueless!"

"What the—"

Then she threw his glasses to the ground and crushed them like a cigarette.

"I don't think so, *honey!*"

Skip, shocked silent, bent down to pick up the wiry mess. "If you value your life, don't mess with a pregnant woman," advised Francie. "So, should I drive?"

And that marked the end of our House Truffles. As much as Francie wanted to, she didn't try to coax Ginger into making them again.

A few weeks later, at the height of Christmas rush—Skip was making a delivery, Ginger had already left as she was working only half shifts—Stella was helping out in the shop and rummaging through her red shoe bag again. All day long she performed her routine of changing out of pumps to sneakers to slippers and back to pumps, bitching the whole time about her arches, her bunions, her varicose veins. Only one thing distracted her from the pain. Craning her neck to look out the window, she paused in her routine. Behind her cat eyeglasses, her left brow suddenly shot up.

"Something snag your eye, Stella?" Francie said, gazing out. "A nice Jewish boy, perhaps?"

Stella, craning her neck: "All I see is Mr. Tall, Dark, and Dreamy in the blue suit and silver tie."

Only one guy in the lobby fit that description. He was African American, handsome, and buff—and about half her age, if that.

"Him?"

"Yes, him."

"Uh, do you think he's old enough for you?"

"Are you joking?"

"Of course I'm joking, Stella!"

"Look, after my husband walked out, screw the rules. I'm too old for them, Francie. Besides, all the men in Leisure World remind me of him. Now, keep your eye out for Mr. Tall, Dark, and Dreamy. And don't get any ideas unless you want a catfight on your hands."

So petite most customers could see only the top of her blond head over the counter, Stella finished changing into her pumps with a wink and a warning. "I can take you, you know."

"I believe you, Stella."

After Christmas, we convinced Stella to leave her job at Naron Candy and work full-time as our manager. We needed a helping hand, what with Ginger expecting a child and our book commitments, and could pay her more than she was making at Naron. Stella, sick to death of driving around the Beltway making sales calls, still dreamed of the day she could stop working and travel the world first-class. But that wasn't going to happen now, or anytime soon. At least our sweetshop offered her a window into a world where she could long for a Mr. Tall, Dark, and Dreamy.

But toward the middle of April when Stella took off from work to entertain her Passover guests, we shared a sisterly work shift, and it was like old times. Ginger was waddling about out front with her Windex and paper towels, big as a boat. The bare-bones shelves needed a good dusting before displaying our Mother's Day offerings. Being here was a pleasure for Ginger, as she was growing restless at home and, besides, Skip was here, and Columbia Hospital for Women was just six blocks away. That morning she'd awoken feeling slightly off and decided to skip her morning trot on the treadmill. Later, while packing up a box of Peanut Butter Smoothies for her first customer, a gentle ping went off in her lower back, like it was trying to tell her something. But she felt fine now, good enough to dust. No matter where she was in the shop, customers apologized for being in her way. She was all baby.

"Thanks," she kept saying.

A woman in a business suit was milling around. Her name badge indicated she was in town for business, probably on lunch break. She couldn't stop yawning.

"Need some help?" Francie wondered.

The woman, yawning yet again, didn't hear her. Only the vision of Ginger in all her pregnant glory revived her.

"My God, how far along are you?"

"Nine months. My due date is in two weeks."

"Whew," joked an eavesdropping male customer, "I was afraid you just put on weight since the last time I saw you."

The whole shop erupted in laughter.

"Do you feel okay?" Ms. Tired inquired. "Because you look like you're about to blow."

"I woke up today feeling like I'm definitely in the final stretch. A couple of pings here and there, but my doctor told me if the contractions don't stop me in my tracks, then keep going on with my day. All in all I'm fine except that I'm chocolate deprived and being here is *killing* me." Ginger laughed.

"Then why aren't you home resting your poor feet?"

"When I'm home, I miss the shop," Ginger expressed, casting a longing look around. She took a mental picture—*snap!*—to keep during her maternity leave. "Plus, our manager took this week off for Passover, so here I am, ready to give birth to my first child any minute."

"Boy or girl?"

"Boy."

"A little boy." Ms. Tired smiled. "How wonderful. I have one, too."

"Aw, how old is he?"

"Twenty-three."

"Oh!"

"He's in graduate school at Cornell. But I remember carrying him like yesterday—and so will you."

Like dear old friends, the two ended up in the Chat Corner talking all things Motherhood from morning sickness to swollen feet to labor pains to dilation to the birthing process to nipple latching. This was called the Instant Club-of-Mothers syndrome. Now Francie was the one yawning, having witnessed this phenomenon countless times before in our store.

"Anybody need help?" she called out.

An hour later, after enduring pings and pangs in her stomach and back, Ginger was in the middle of helping Edgar when she felt something go down her leg. Was it . . . a trickle of water? Nah.

Edgar was taking his sweet time choosing chocolates today. It seemed that whenever someone on his Christmas list passed away, he would come in to report it, in no hurry to rush back to the world of investments. Linger with his loss. We understood, and as far as we were concerned, he could stay all day, every day. Edgar was usually the gift giver, but today, damn it, he was treating himself.

"Life is too short for deprivation," he stated, smacking his lips. "I'm craving something, but I don't know what. Do you ever feel that way, Ginger?"

"Edgar, you have no idea."

"This looks interesting," he noted, face in the case. "Have you ever tried the Manon Noir?"

"Only about a million of them," Ginger replied, recalling the flavor of dark chocolate mousse with a swirl of milk chocolate on top—rapture in one bite. She was still musing when a second trickle down her leg quickly chased her daydream away.

"Sorry, Edgar, but I have to excuse myself."

"Are you all right?"

"Yes, but Skip needs to take over for me," she said. "Skip, can you please help Edgar?"

"Sure thing."

Ginger waddled into the back room with Francie on her trail—literally. "Oh, my God," she said as she leaned on her sister, "look down!"

A puddle of water collected on the floor. Francie freaked—there really *was* a baby in there.

"Skip! Skip! Ginger's water broke!"

On the evening of April 14, 1998, Ginger gave birth to a baby boy they named Justin. Oddly, there was no Skip in the baby's face.

"He looks just like you," Skip proudly assessed. For once, his smile was bigger than his 'stache.

Ginger, cradling the baby so tightly all Skip could do was marvel and take pictures, corrected him. "He looks just like Dad." Her breast rose and fell. "I wish you could've met your grandfather," she whispered to her infant son. "He would've loved you so much."

"Amen," Skip said.

Only when Francie and Mom were allowed into the hospital room, a giant box of milk and dark chocolates in tow, did Ginger's grip loosen. Pecan and Cashew Turtles, Almond Bark, a smattering of Nonpareils and Fraises des Bois—all her favorites. Was it her imagination, or did the hospital room already smell like our shop?

Francie squeezed her hand. "How do you feel?"

"Exhausted but good."

"He's beautiful, Ginge."

"Here, Grandma," Skip said, "say hello to your grandson."

Mom rocked him. "Sorry, Skip, he don't look like you. He look like my husband."

"Just wait until he grows a mustache," Skip joked. "Hey, Francie, my son's making the rounds and it's your turn to hold him."

"In a minute, Skip."

He delivered the baby back to Ginger. "Okay, but you're going to regret this if you're planning to wait until he's in the NFL."

Unable to hold back any longer, Ginger cried, "How long do I have to wait? Gimme my chocolate!"

"Sorry, Ginge, I forgot," Francie said, opening up the box. "You deserve every piece in here after what you've gone through. Skip"—she slapped his hand away—"no chocolate for you!"

"And who made you the Chocolate Nazi?"

"CHOCOLATE!" Ginger was yelling.

A beautiful exchange: a box of chocolates for a bundle of joy.

Francie was breathless. Babies were foreign objects to her. What do you do with them? Say to them? Do they break?

"Justin," Ginger said, turning him over to her big sister, "I want you to meet your aunt."

And then it happened: Francie took Justin from Ginger and held him in her arms. When Justin peed all over Francie, she exhaled with so much love it hurt, "He's a prince!"

Meanwhile, we were fast closing in on the eve of the publication of our children's book *My Freedom Trip: A Child's Escape from North Korea*. Our publisher was hosting a reception in our honor at the National Press Club in June. But our excitement was dampened by heart-wrenching news.

Ginger was home writing thank-you notes to the many customers who showered her with baby gifts when an odd letter came in the mail.

"Who's it from?" she asked Mom.

"Long-lost relative who live in California."

The last time they had seen each other was in Korea before the war broke out. They were schoolgirls then, distantly related, and Mom could hardly remember her. When she opened up the letter, a black-and-white photograph fell out.

"*Oma*," she cried.

It was a picture of her mother somewhere in North Korea, evidently taken on her sixtieth birthday, her *hwan-gap*, the most celebrated of all Korean birthdays. The hwan-gap was a time of much fanfare and bountiful goods lined up banquet style—even the poorest people somehow managed to scrape together a feast fit for a king or queen, if just for one day. But her mother's celebration was nothing more than a few stringed figs. Saddest of all was the expression on her face, so grief-stricken no daughter should see it.

"Mom, where did this so-called relative get this?"

Eyes vacant, Mom pressed the photograph to her chest and began to tremble. "Not sure."

"I don't understand . . ."

"What it matter, anyway? Letter say my mother go blind and die."

"No, Mom, no . . ."

"She . . . starve to death."

Mom began to weep.

All those Hershey bars Mom nibbled on in her suburban Virginia kitchen while floating off into her own foreign world—had they simply been leading to this discovery?

"*Oma*," she kept crying.

The timing couldn't be more eerie.

When our author copies of My *Freedom Trip* were delivered to our headquarters, Mom couldn't look at the book. For her, the carton they came in was a coffin and every glossy page a nightmarish reminder that the defining story of her life did not have a happy ending.

"Don't show to me. Don't read."

Yet somehow, like her character in the book, Mom put on a heroic face at our reception, and it was easy to forget it was all an act.

"Yes, thank you! Yes, true story, my story . . . !"

Bowing from an ancient era, Mom greeted a ballroom of friends and customers who showed up to offer their support, one by one. The Bear, Edgar, Stella, Carol, Bill-About-Town, and even Stan the UPS man were among the five hundred guests.

"What a party," Ginger exclaimed.

"Imagine if Dad were here," Francie said.

After a short speech, we signed books until our hands cramped. When Skip finally arrived with Justin in his BabyBjörn, the picture was almost complete.

Through a crowd enjoying bubbly and fancy little plates of food, Francie gazed out looking for a floppy hat. Where was Gypsy Bess? She had said she would try to make it, but by evening's end, it was apparent she was a no-show.

Guests were filing out of the ballroom when Mom said, "We go now."

The minute we stepped on the elevator, Mom's brave face all but disappeared.

"Are you okay?" we asked her, escorting her to the car.

Mom nodded, unable to speak. On the ride home, not one word. It wasn't until we got home that the woman who for fifty years, in the comfort of her suburban American life, had hoped against hope that her mother was spared suffering on the other side of the globe, collapsed. No matter what we said to her that night, she was somewhere so far away she couldn't hear us, couldn't understand our language. We could only hold her hand and listen to her cry.

The following day, Gypsy Bess showed up. In flowing tie-dye, purple beads, and huge hoop earrings, she ambled toward the shop. Somehow she seemed slower than usual. Skip sprinted to open the door for her.

"Thanks, Skip. What are the celebs doing here with the rest of us worker bees?"

We crooned our familiar tune: "Doing what we love."

"Which means being around chocolate and giving me hell," Skip wisecracked.

In the Chat Corner, Gypsy Bess apologized to Francie for not making an appearance at the National Press Club. "Getting around isn't as easy as it used to be. I was thinking of you, though."

"I know you were, Bess. Hey, let's get a cup of coffee."

"I can't, darlin', I have to go back to the office to clean out my desk."

"Why?"

Gypsy Bess's tie-dyed bosom heaved up then down. "Francie"—she paused—"my breast cancer's back."

"No . . ."

"Yes, and I came by today to say good-bye."

"Good-bye?"

"Now, don't worry about me. I beat breast cancer before, and I'll beat it again. But I need to be near my kids and my granddaughter Ashley, who I miss like the dickens. I love D.C. and Old Town, and God knows I've loved my independence for the past twelve years, but who am I kidding? It's getting too hard for me to take care of myself. West Virginia, here I come, right back where I started from."

"But Bess, we'll take care of you. We'll help you beat this. And after you're all better, if you need groceries or just want company, Ginger and I are here for you. If you need muscles, Skip's always at your service, you know that."

"I can't ask you to do those things for me. I can't and I won't. I'm too proud and that's probably been my problem my whole life, but nothing's going to change that now. Now, not another word about me. I want to hear about you. How's your love life?"

Francie shrugged. Who cared at a time like this? "I was seeing that one guy."

"You mean the columnist?"

"Yes."

"He's not chocolate-worthy," she snapped.

"Why not?"

"He's Republican, not worth your *writing interruptus*."

Amused: "I guess I'm just more in love with books."

"That's fine and dandy, and I sure did enjoy reading your story about the baker and her perfect cake, but you still need lovin'. Tell me, Francie, how do you see yourself in years to come?"

No need to ponder. "I know it sounds crazy, Bess, but once I'm done with the high heels, I've always pictured myself as a little old lady with a long silvery white braid, living in a log cabin in Cape Cod. It's winter and I've got a fire going."

"Is there a man in that cozy little scene?"

"I don't know."

"More important, is there chocolate?"

"Well, of course." Gypsy Bess knew what mattered.

"Take it from an old broad who's liberated enough to know that you don't need a man, but if you have one, even if he's in the cabin next door, it would make that fire roar, darlin'. When I divorced Joe, I was sure I was doing the right thing and a part of me still is. But sometimes I think I didn't slow down to think things through, to imagine life ahead without him. All I'm saying is that you should have more sweet times in your life, Francie. Find a guy who'll wash your hair and listen to you read and cook for you. That's what I wish for you from the bottom of my heart. Now I'm growing sad and I've got to get going. Please say good-bye to your mama for me. I love you, darlin'. Will you ever come visit me in Charleston?"

"I will."

Gypsy Bess hugged each of us good-bye, then walked out of our shop for the last time. Watching her figure growing smaller in the lobby until only a floppy hat distinguished her from the crowd, Francie, already fearing the finery of her friend would fade in her mind's eye, made a promise to herself.

"I'm going to write about you, Bess, starting tonight."

❦ Chapter 16 ❧

Dark Almond Bark

*Slabs of dark chocolate with toasted
whole almonds*

We blinked, and it was a new millennium.

The look of Chocolate Chocolate had changed, reflecting our changing lives. Even as we were living it, it felt like our Golden Era.

We'd invested in sprucing up the place with more sparkling mirrors plus a granite countertop to showcase our German marzipan bars and figurines. On a new two-tiered table out front sat old-fashioned confectionary jars filled with chocolate-covered morsels, there for the sampling and scooping—toffee, almonds, coffee beans, you name it, they were all-natural, all pop-in-the-mouth addictive, and whenever a customer forgot to put a lid back on, its lovely incense wafted through the air.

"Love the new look," quipped Bill-About-Town, munching on

the last of his Chocolate-Covered Pretzels. Only two today—he had a plane to catch.

"Where you headed this time, Bill?" Francie quizzed him, noticing a pinch of salt in his beard. "Off to Hong Kong, the Taj Mahal, or Paris?"

When Bill traveled, he always had something else up his sleeve. Interviewing locals, photographing sunsets, comparing cafés.

"Nope, just to New York," he said, crumpling up his bag and taking aim at our trash can behind the counter. Point! "Gotta go, but nice job here, guys. The shop looks amazing."

As the shop evolved, so did its microcosm of life. While new customers walked in, some often enough to warrant nicknames, like the Southern Belle who breezily popped by for gifts and the Good Son who was always on the hunt for Mom chocolates, others walked out forever. Lulu—Ms. Gratitude—brought us orchids the day before moving back to Honolulu, with a note that said "Long Live Bittersweet Chocolate—Mahalo." Most customers said goodbye before leaving town, but some silently slunk away and it wouldn't be until one of us said something like, "Hey, where did So-and-So go?" that we'd realize So-and-So was gone. And Bulldog? By now he'd faded from the picture, perhaps stalking a harem of exotic dancers in another club in another city. Meanwhile, settled back in West Virginia, Gypsy Bess won her second battle with breast cancer. And the Bear, who began our friendship with a chocolate shamrock, left us too; he was now living in Brooklyn and working in his company's Manhattan office.

Years of quiet writing struggles were coming to fruition. Together and apart, we'd written numerous novels and children's books, most embracing our family heritage and the Asian-American experience. Some even got published and ended up sharing shelf space with beautiful boxed chocolates. All day long, customers remarked, "Books and chocolate—what a perfect fit."

We thanked our lucky stars for the books that made big splashes and made peace with the ones that didn't. In the end, being authors offered us the same wealth as being shopkeepers: a whirlwind of life experiences to keep forever.

And indeed, April 4, 2000, was a day we would never forget. We, along with millions of people, tuned in to *Good Morning America*, though not as casual viewers. The week before, ABC correspondent Juju Chang had flown down from New York at dawn to interview us about our multicultural writing, and specifically about Francie's just-released novel, *When My Sister Was Cleopatra Moon*, about a Korean family in 1970s white suburbia. Juju and her crew descended on our headquarters, the home Dad provided for us with big hopes and dreams for all his children. Here we are, Dad. Are you watching? Yet as the camera crew positioned spotlights to set up a mock stage, the living room bore little resemblance to the room where he would come to unwind from a long day, waxing on about Tolstoy and smoking his pipe. We were awed by the lights, the equipment, the immediacy of it, as we watched the setup from the doorway.

"Ginge," Francie psssted, knowing she was up first, "my mind's a complete blank."

"Join the club."

"Do I look okay?"

"Fine. What about me?"

"Divine."

We were seated and ready to go, but as soon as the cameras started rolling, Francie's arms went up like a traffic cop's. "Stop, I'm going to say something stupid, I can feel it."

"They'll edit it out," everyone assured her.

When it was Ginger's turn to talk, jitters got the best of her and she couldn't get the words out. "Cut, cut!"

A week later, the moment had come: Our segment was airing after the commercial break. We'd been on local television, but, c'mon, this was the whole damn country.

Shouting, Mom nearly jumped off the couch. "Look!"

Flashing on the TV screen was a black-and-white photograph superimposed on the Times Square marquee.

"Your daddy took that picture!"

Yes, on a mountainside, circa 1964, one summer day so long ago: Big Sis, Little Sis, Mom.

Too soon the image was replaced by a current image of two women waiting on customers in a sweetshop.

"My girls," Mom sang.

Hands over our faces, we watched Diane Sawyer and Charlie Gibson introduce the segment, gradually letting our hands go so we could watch it all. Though a well-done piece, the unflattering camera angles left Francie cringing.

"I'm going into therapy," she announced.

Our interview the next year with Diane Rehm for our coauthored book *To Swim Across the World*, a fictionalized account of our parents' experiences as young people during Korea's most turbulent era—a piano-playing girl from the north, a milk boy from the south—was no less harried. Stage fright had seized us on the drive over to American University's WAMU studio. Francie kept coughing and Ginger got a terrible tickle in her throat.

"I can't go on." Francie coughed.

"Me either."

"This is live radio!"

When Diane Rehm walked into the studio, our anxieties melted away. Beauty and calm radiated from her, inside and out. Humor, too.

"Where's my chocolate?" she said.

Was it all really happening?

Yes, and while it was, it was as if our minds were filming so we could rewind the reels for the rest of our lives. And at every venue from CNN to the Smithsonian to Wolf Trap, the topic of books inevitably turned to chocolate. At every school visit from Pinewood Elementary in Timonium, Maryland, to Keene Mill Elementary in Springfield, Virginia, every class somehow managed to steer all talk of books to "CHOCOLATE!"

In the summer of 2001, we went on a West Coast book tour, which took us three thousand miles out of our comfort zone. We were homesick before the plane landed in Seattle.

Ginger sighed into her seat, aching all over. "I miss Justin."

Justin was a young prince with an old soul. Like Dad, he demonstrated a gift for language. Long before he could talk, he could arrange his ABC letters and identify any video from a huge homemade collection we taped and hand-labeled.

"Justin, grab Blue's Clues Birthday," we'd say.

He would crawl over. Grab the video. Hold it up with a pudgy paw. It was mind-blowing. Sometimes it was like catching glimpses of Justin in the future, but inevitably he would spit up and lapse into babyhood again. But now he was a big boy, three years old.

"I miss him, too," Francie grieved. "He's my little fate mate."

Ever since Ginger got back into the tennis swing of things, Francie had been reveling in her stolen time with Justin on Sunday mornings. They read books and watched Nickelodeon; they ran around the house and then fell asleep, side by side, on the couch. When Ginger got back, she'd launch into a descriptive minute-by-minute playback as if Francie could understand a word of tennis lingo.

We were going to be away from our little routines for only one week, but it was still hard.

"I miss Mom." Ginger sighed some more.

"And her cooking."

"I even miss ole Chubby Hubby."

"Let's call them when we land."

Meanwhile, Skip was manning the shop with Stella while Mom looked after her grandson.

"I try read book to him but he read book to me!"

We couldn't help wondering: Did his future lie in books as well? One thing was for certain, it did *not* lie in chocolate. Justin had severe allergies to milk, nuts, sesame, and eggs, and sometimes even being in the shop made him break out in hives. So much for our kid in our candy store. Since we spent many of our days off playing with him and thinking up special recipes for him, Justin managed to do something we didn't think was humanly possible: tighten our bond.

Across the country, in San Francisco's Fisherman's Wharf area, we were just two visitors out of thousands checking out the festive sights. Then, Francie heard something. She stopped so suddenly in her tracks that the people behind us bumped into each other, creating a minor traffic jam.

"Did you hear that, Ginge?"

"I think so, but . . . it couldn't be . . ."

We kept walking when suddenly a couple in a car moving slowly in traffic on the narrow road stuck their heads out.

"Chocolate Chocolate!" they called out in unison. "We know you girls from Washington, D.C.!"

Although we couldn't see them well enough to recognize them, we waved back like long-lost friends. Missing our daily routines even more, we did the next best thing and headed toward Ghirardelli Square. At their candy shop, we snatched up a clutch of foiled chocolate squares and were promptly rung up by a young cashier, an Asian-American girl with a sweet round face.

Ginger exchanged a wink with her sister. "Now we've got a little taste of home."

There was something to be said for being outside on a magnificent day near the water and eating chocolates. Thin, small, and snappy, the mint ones made us very happy.

Out of nowhere, Francie said, "Were we ever that young?"

"As who?"

"The cashier."

Ginger smiled. "Once."

The next week, back in D.C., we couldn't wait to get back to the shop and into the swing of things. Rejoin our own ranks! When a woman in bookworm specs stepped in, looking a bit frazzled, Ginger beat Stella to her, greeting her with a winning smile.

"Hi, what can I help you find today?"

"I need a quick fix of dark chocolate," she pleaded. "I'm new to town, so this is my first time in. Tell me what you've got."

Responding to desperation, Ginger quickly ran down a quick list of our highlights when the woman interrupted her.

"Dark Chocolate Orange Peel! I'll take a quarter pound. Sorry to be in such a rush, but I've got to get back to my office right away. I've got a million things on my mind, you know? But, wow, this is a nice store. I'll be back."

Francie gave her a warm smile. "Promise?"

Nodding, the woman popped a piece in her mouth and crumpled her bag up, ready to go. But once she got into the chew of dark chocolate and candied orange peel, she slowed down, as if the million things on her mind floated away.

"I'm definitely having a chocolate moment here," she said.

As other customers came in and we assisted them, the woman lingered, eating more orange peel and browsing. In time her eyes landed on something that caused her to remove her specs for closer examination. When the place cleared out, she inquired; "Why are those books on the shelf?"

"My sister and I wrote them together," Ginger replied simply.

"You're kidding!"

"No, why?"

She held out her hand and introduced herself. "I'm Nancy. I just moved down from New York to head up the children's book division at National Geographic. I'm their new editorial director."

Ginger's eyes widened while Francie shook her hand. "Don't you love serendipity?"

Nancy nodded. "I came in looking for chocolate and found two authors. Let's talk *very* soon." She grabbed a business card before dashing out of our shop.

The wittiest politico in Washington, the Senator, held the door open for Nancy. With striking silver hair, the Senator was an old-school Southern gent with surprisingly progressive views. Indeed, his only scandalous behavior was counting Chocolate-Dipped Apricots as his fruit serving for the day.

"I'll take six of my favorites, doll," he said to Ginger.

"Brace yourself, Senator, the price on the Apricots has gone up. That'll be thirteen dollars and twenty-five cents."

"Why, that's more than the mortgage on my first house," he hollered at her with comical outrage. When he spotted Skip, he mumbled out of the corner of his mouth, "Someone decided to get off the couch today." Addressing Skip directly: "This is the first time I've actually seen you in the shop, Skip. For the longest time, I thought you worked at Starbucks."

Skip, always hopeful for some juicy insider talk, chuckled. "Hey, Senator, what do you think of the North Korean president visiting Russia and meeting with President Putin?"

"Lots, but I've got a cab waiting, Skip. Let's talk tomorrow. Think you might make it into work, or is two days in a row too much for you?"

"Senator," Francie informed him, "he's always in."

"He is?"

Ginger smirked. "Well, what she means is that he's here, hiding in the back."

Skip shot her a look.

"Don't hide too much, Skip." The Senator smiled. "I have a good friend I think you'd enjoy talking to."

Skip was intrigued. "Really?"

"One of these days I'll bring him by."

At opening hour the next day, an e-mail popped up from a local school we were visiting later on that week. Their librarian, Miss Kendall, was sending us a list of students whose parents were pre-ordering our books, along with requested inscriptions.

"Not a very long list," Ginger noted.

Francie got out two pens and lamented, "That's because many of the students here are considered at-risk."

"You know what that means."

"Longer hugs from the kids."

While we were busy autographing books at the counter, Stella was on the lookout. She still had an eye for Tall, Dark, and Dreamy men.

"Girls," she psssted, all eyes, "girls!"

This particular Mr. Tall, Dark, and Dreamy looked kindly at Stella, like she was a little old grandma.

"Good morning." He nodded.

Winking back: "My, don't you look dapper today."

"Why, thank you. I was wondering—"

"The answer is yes, I have whatever you want, whenever you want. And if you don't know what you want, I'll tell you what you want."

Listening in was a matronly mother who had slipped in with three boys, ranging from tween to teen. The mother asked her, "Have you seen the film *Chocolat*?"

Stella huffed. "Why bother, dear? I'm living it."

Mr. Tall, Dark, and Dreamy, who didn't realize that Stella was flirting with him—madly—was amused. "What a great attitude you have, ma'am."

"Please, I don't look old enough to be a *ma'am*, do I?"

He laughed like they were playing a game. "Well, of course not."

Ginger put down a book to help the mother and her sons. "Hi, there, how are you all doing today?"

"Wonderful!"

Francie cast a quick glance, still signing. "Nice day to be out and about, isn't it?"

"Yes," the mother agreed, half smiling like she was keeping a secret. "I haven't been here in so long."

Our smiles back must've been blank.

"You ladies don't remember me, do you?"

There *was* something familiar about her. The inflection of her voice? The crinkle of her nose?

Finally, she blushed. "I used to stop in here every Friday night after work on my way to Philadelphia. But this was way back in the eighties."

Flash back to a young lady in a red coat . . . It was Our Girl Friday, all grown up! She was older now, of course, with vague resemblance to her Audrey Hepburn silhouette of 1984. But even if we didn't want to admit it, we'd all changed. Stella wasn't the only one being called *ma'am* these days, and unlike the way we used to feel, like girls in a city of grown-ups, our customers were looking younger and younger to us. In case there was any doubt, all we had to do was look at Skip's silver mustache.

After exchanging pleasantries, and thanking her for stopping in and making our day, the mother we once knew as Our Girl Friday said it was time to leave. "We're supposed to meet my husband at the Corcoran." For old times' sake, she purchased the same ring-sized box she always bought, and then, with her three sons, slipped out the door once again.

"Next time we see her," we said wistfully, "she'll be a grandmother."

At closing hour, an e-mail from Editor Nancy popped up: *Great to meet you two yesterday. I was wondering whether you would happen to have a coming-to-America story in your family. If so, let me know. I'd love to work with you. Nancy*

But in the midst of this Golden Era, more golden than two dreaming sisters could ever have imagined:

9/11.

Like so many across the country, we were frantic about the people we knew in New York. That afternoon we tried contacting our old friend, the Bear, lover of Dark Almond Bark, who had relocated to the city some time ago. Hours later, we finally got word from his son that, unlike so many of his colleagues, he escaped the collapse of the Second World Trade Center where he worked. Our relief was palpable, and yet bittersweet, in the midst of such incredible loss. Maybe, just maybe, we told ourselves, the chocolate shamrock he purchased years ago brought him good luck, too.

Besides the horror of what had happened, we were uncertain how to proceed with our business. In the wake of such tragedy, we had no idea what to expect. Was anyone in the mood for chocolate? Should we even open for business? Was it safe to come into the city?

There was only one way to find out. The next day we made the decision to resume business. Police blocked our usual route, past the Pentagon and over the Memorial Bridge, so we followed the traffic over the 14th Street Bridge.

A steady stream of customers came in that day. Like us, they were shell-shocked and subdued, seeking solace in our shop. The same sentiment kept ringing over and over.

"I need comfort chocolates."

Comfort chocolates. Now we understood why Mom once nibbled on black-market chocolates at a time when her next breath could be her last. Halfway around the globe, a half century later, our customers were feeling the very same way.

"I could eat this stuff forever," declared a businessman holding a slab of Dark Almond Bark as big as his hand.

A woman, exhausted with the state of the world, nodded. "Pack me up a pound of that, ladies."

After Ginger packed her box, she handed it to her with a sad smile.

"Thank you," the customer said, leaving to go. At the door she turned around and held up her bag. "You know, if you handed this out in a war zone, there'd be peace on earth."

The rest of 2001 wore on. Soon after her e-mail query, Editor Nancy commissioned us to write a coming-to-America story for National Geographic Books. Exciting—yet it was impossible to feel truly joyful in the days and months following 9/11. Ginger hugged Justin longer and tighter whenever she dropped him off at pre-school; Francie spent more time than ever with Mom, going for long rides on the weekends to scenic places like Harpers Ferry and Skyline Drive where the world felt safer, if only for a few hours. Luckily for us, people continued to come into the shop, taking comfort in chocolate. But a tinge of the atmosphere—the gaiety or innocence, perhaps the purity of it—had changed. At year's end, the city was still shell-shocked and subdued.

Chapter 17

Chocolate-Dipped Graham

*That famous sweet cracker
coated in chocolate—love that snap!*

Stella was crashing. At five o'clock on Valentine's Day, we all were. The later in the week the official day of love fell, the madder the crush, and in 2002, it fell on a Thursday. This was our nineteenth Valentine's Day at Chocolate Chocolate, but some things hadn't changed. Need to eat, sneeze, go to the ladies' room? Forget about it.

"I can't hold it any longer," Stella said, rummaging through her shoe bag. "This girdle's about to blow."

Our Stella refused to step foot in public wearing flats. "Men like swagger," was her line, "and if I run into a Mr. Tall, Dark, and Dreamy, I better have it." That said, even a quick trip down the escalator to the ladies' room meant puttin' on the pumps.

As she was leaving, Skip squinted. "Looking a little wobbly

over there, Stella. Why don't you wait a sec and we can go down together?"

Appalled: "I don't need an escort, Skip. Don't fuss over me like I'm an old lady."

Back, poor Stella was left banging and yelling for a good ten minutes outside our back room.

"Open up, open up, I forgot my key."

"Hold on, Stella," we kept calling out to her. Swamped with customers, it was hard to catch a break.

When Francie finally opened the door, she was taken aback. Stella's fluffy hair was cotton candy, and there was something unsteady about her.

"Are you okay?"

"I'm fine, darling."

"Whatever you do, Stella," Francie started, cracking up, "don't look down."

Which Stella did, of course.

"Oh, my Gawd!"

Ginger dropped her tongs and stuck her head in the back. "What's going on?"

Stella, beet-red, pointed down to a pair of mismatched feet: a black pump on one foot, a red sneaker on the other.

"So much for swagger," she quipped.

Unfortunately, Valentine's Day didn't end on such a funny note. At the Farragut North Metro, a young man in a rush to catch a train knocked into Stella with such force she was thrown to the ground. The man stopped only long enough to ask her if she was all right, then hopped onto the train before the doors closed. Other riders helped her up.

"I'm fine, I'm fine," Stella told them.

But she wasn't. Both her hips, worn with age, had been nagging her for some time, but now her left hip, the one she fell on, seriously hurt. Although Stella managed to hobble behind the counter with us for a few weeks longer, eventually she had no choice but to undergo hip replacement surgery.

"I'll be back to work in six months and not a day later," she promised us with every fiber of her being.

But shortly after Stella's surgery, her doctor recommended her right hip be replaced as well. She broke the news to us over lo mein noodles when we visited her in her Leisure World apartment. We brought Justin along, now four, who was playing with Stella's grandsons.

"It turns out Dr. Jacobs knew it all along," she said between slurps. "He just didn't have the heart to tell me earlier. God, I miss being where the action is."

What a blow, to all of us. We couldn't imagine shop life without Stella, yet we couldn't help but wonder: Was she really ever coming back? With our book engagements—school visits and book readings all over the metropolitan area—and numerous works in progress, we had no choice but to find a replacement for our beloved employee.

But who? No one could take her place.

"I'll be back," Stella swore, fist to the sky, "you can't get rid of me that easily."

Enter Koomo, a tennis buddy of Ginger's, bestowing advice about our newly launched authors' Web site.

"Ginger, I cannot tell a lie. Your Web site's drab and doesn't draw you in, nothing is set up right . . ."

Francie, back from a coffee break, knew exactly who he was. At thirty-four, the Greek guy's blondness and slight frame would allow him to pass for a college kid. Ginger was always telling stories about her quirky friend, and on this day in May, his "Peanuts" Christmas tie proved that. Ginger introduced them.

"Hi, Koomo," Francie said, "I've heard a lot about you."

He looked right through her. "So, Ginger, all settled in the new house?"

Not long ago, Ginger and Skip had bought the home of their dreams. Mom followed. Leaving Dad's castle and the place we called our headquarters was eased by the fact that they moved only three miles away. We would still drive by our yellow Colonial, though Mom got furious when she saw that the new owners had cut down Dad's willow tree in the front yard.

"Why they do that? Shouldn't sell to them."

Francie, at the wheel, driving slowly. "I guess it's their house now, Mom."

"So, need a housewarming gift?" Koomo was asking Ginger.

"Whatcha got?"

"Hot pepper plants and mo' hot pepper plants."

Francie was slightly annoyed at being ignored, but she figured he was just a weirdo.

"A lovable one, though," Ginger later qualified.

Well, if Ginger was so amused by him, he couldn't be all bad.

In June, he was back talking to Ginger. Francie stayed in the background, listening—the guy was free entertainment. Wearing a tie patterned with Tabasco bottles, Koomo said he'd just been laid off from his job as an events planner for some public affairs association on K Street.

Ginger was concerned. "What are you going to do?"

"Go home and brush up on my Middle English," he said. Giving us a taste of a strange mumbo-jumbo tongue, he began to recite:

"Ther nys no thyng superlatif as lyveth . . ." Ginger avoided eye contact with Francie. Koomo went on, becoming more theatrical and nonsensical. But soon stumbling, he halted. "As you can tell, I'm rusty."

After he left, Francie couldn't help laughing. "Is he for real?"

"Believe it or not."

In July, Koomo was back in the shop, obviously unemployed, in shorts and a Cure T-shirt. Francie wondered what this visit would bring.

"I come bearing gifts." He held up two baggies of homegrown hot peppers. Red, yellow, green, and brown, long and thin peppers and short and squat ones. "Here, Ginger."

"Thanks, Koomo, these are gorgeous."

"One for you and one for your mom."

"We can chop 'em up and do a million things with them. Hey, this one looks like chocolate."

"Duh, it's a chocolate habañero."

"Aha."

"You know, you could make a fortune selling hot peppers covered with chocolate."

"Noted, Koomo."

"Francie," he spoke out of nowhere, "I would've brought you some, too, but Ginger told me you're not into hot peppers."

Her wry reply startled him. "Oh, so you finally decided to acknowledge me?"

Koomo apologized. "I'm a social goon. Besides, Ginger talks about you so much, I know everything about you."

"Oh, God."

"And since peppers are my passion, I have one question I've been meaning to ask you."

"What's that?"

"Why can't you take the heat?"

Afterward, Francie noted, "He's got unusual social skills, Ginge."

Studying her bag of peppers: "Are you thinking what I'm thinking?"

"I think so. Let's hire him."

Whenever Sherry the Southern Belle swept in, she brought with her the fresh outdoors, be it a spring day in April or a summer day in August, which it was now. With her deep Savannah drawl, she loved to chat as if we were all sipping lemonades on a green lawn. Poking around for gifts for her friends and family was a thoughtful activity for Sherry, and she was always drawn to our chocolate collectibles that varied from one season to another. Pairing the perfect figurine for the perfect recipient took a little time, and her time seemed to be her own. That day chocolate fish, golf balls, flowers, and globes were among our novelties.

"Hi, y'all," she said as she swept in. "Did everyone have a nice weekend?"

The Southern Belle always had time to talk before she started shopping.

Koomo mulled. "I listened to the Cure in the Tree House," he said, as if the whole world knew the Tree House was his condo, "so, yeah, it was a nice weekend."

"What's the Cure?"

Stepping back, Koomo, hands on hips, pretended to be appalled. "Shame on you for not knowing who the Cure is, Sherry."

"Uh-oh, I think I'm in trouble, people."

"They're an English rock band."

"And is the Tree House a club or something?"

"Actually, it's my condo."

Trying to inject a bit of normalcy, Ginger explained, "His condo overlooks a park and when you're up there, looking out his windows, you literally feel like you're in the trees."

"I see. Well"—Sherry clapped—"my definition of the Cure is chocolate. And I need to buy a present for my daughter. She needs a little cheering up. You know, young love."

So the Southern Belle had a daughter. We had pictured her as a lady of leisure and now edited our vision of her to include a family.

"Not really," replied Koomo, who had begun working for us a week after toting in the bags o' peppers. "I'm waiting for the girl of my dreams to walk in."

"Not yet, Koomo?"

"Not yet."

"Sherry, what about a chocolate heart?" Francie suggested.

With a leap, Koomo was already out front in search of one to show her, face to heart. "Like this, maybe?"

Sherry pondered. "A sweet thought, but I suspect my daughter might just break it in two."

"A chocolate butterfly, maybe?" Ginger suggested. "The pink one's the prettiest."

"No, the yellow," Francie cooed.

"Well, I like the purple butterfly." Koomo plucked one from a garden of chocolate butterflies on the bottom shelf. Once he placed it in Sherry the Southern Belle's hand, she grew contemplative.

"You know what? My daughter would love a chocolate ladybug, so I'm getting that for her. But there is someone I know who needs a chocolate butterfly."

A week later Sherry dropped by again.

"Just wanted to tell you guys that my daughter *loved* the chocolate ladybug," she said as her cell phone started ringing. "Excuse me, folks . . ." Her face went dead serious, "Yes, speaking. I'll be in New York by two and we'll go over the deposition . . ." She whispered to us before stepping outside, "Excuse me, but this is work on the phone."

Work? Maybe our instincts were wrong. Maybe Sherry the Southern Belle wasn't a lady of leisure at all.

Another week later Sherry, balancing a high stack of papers, was laughing as she came through the door. Plopping her paperwork on the counter, she went straight for the basket of chocolate ladybugs.

"Can you believe it, people? I'm here to buy another one."

"Oh, no," Ginger began, "don't tell us your daughter's brokenhearted again."

"No, thank goodness, but her best friend's crying her eyes out over some Duke boy—I hear they're good at breaking hearts."

"Is her friend cute?" Koomo wondered.

"Well, of course, she's cute," she replied, "she's twenty years old." Laughter fell like a summer shower.

Francie rang up Sherry's sale, noting her papers. "Looks like you have your work cut out for you."

"Lord, that's an understatement."

"So what is it you do, exactly?"

"I'm a criminal prosecutor."

"No, really?"

"Yes. I crush, kill, and destroy the big bad guys in court." She handed Francie her credit card. "And let me tell you, I have a helluva good time doing it."

Ah, brought to our attention, we could see a glimpse of the steely conviction beneath the sweet exterior. No matter, she'd always be our sweet Southern Belle.

"Thank God you're on our side, Sherry."

"People, I'm always on the side of chocolate," she said, passing Editor Nancy on the way out.

The two women shared a certain nod: the nod of chocolate sisterhood.

"That's my kind of woman," Editor Nancy said, handing us our spanking new children's book, *Good-bye, 382 Shin Dang Dong*. "Congratulations, ladies, hot off the press."

Here was the fruit of our labor. It was beautiful and caught the light as she handed it over. This book recounted our family's coming-to-America story. Unlike some manuscripts that we had struggled with, pulled our hair out over, even thrown away, this one came out in one fell swoop, as if we were under the spell of monsoon rains.

"I'm thrilled," Nancy said.

While we marveled over the illustrations, Nancy reminded us that the Korean artist had flown to Seoul to paint the actual home our parents and older sister left behind in 1954.

Francie turned a page. "Thanks for walking this over, Nancy."

Ginger turned a page. "That's what I call personal service."

To which Editor Nancy smiled and shrugged. "Look, girls, who am I kidding? I'm here for the Dark Chocolate Orange Peel."

With our family's story now recorded and immortalized in a book, the holidays that year took on a certain amount of nostalgia. *A Charlie Brown Christmas* was playing, courtesy of Koomo, of course.

Our mood was poetic as yet another dusk settled on the shop

like snow from our first Christmas here. A poignant silhouette: two sisters, still filling up trays of chocolates, still thinking of their father.

"How many Christmases does this make, Ginge?"

"I don't think I can count that high."

Skip had left early to take Justin to his violin lesson—his Christmas recital was coming up. Koomo was gone, too, off to a Greek church "singles" night, which his mother had begged him to go to. Go, go, we ushered them both out the door. After all these years, we could wait on customers blindfolded. Besides, we craved a little sister time. And chocolate.

"Here," Francie said, cracking off a corner of a Bittersweet Chocolate-Dipped Graham cracker.

Ginger let it sit on her tongue. Once its bittersweet tang zipped through her, she bit down for the sweet cracker snap. There, that was the good part.

Soon she murmured, "Guess it's closing time."

"Okay . . . wait, who is that?"

A limo had pulled up to the curb and the driver who got out looked like he was headed our way. Even with poor night vision, Francie thought there was something haunting about the figure.

"It's Chauffeur Geoffrey!" Ginger exclaimed.

"I'd been wondering about Kahlua Lady," Francie said, getting out a box to fill up. "It's been awhile."

When Geoffrey stepped in, Ginger greeted him. "We knew she couldn't get through the holidays without her truffles."

His face was grim.

"What's wrong?" she asked.

Francie looked up from her half-filled box. "Is Kahlua Lady okay?"

"No, I'm afraid not."

We froze.

"She passed away on Thanksgiving Day. Her husband asked me to stop by here and let you ladies know."

After Geoffrey left, we locked up, turned off both the lights and A *Charlie Brown Christmas*. The world fell silent, as did we.

In the dark, our thoughts flickered back to our early encounters with Kahlua Lady. The first time we addressed her as such, her stately silvery head went back like a prized mare, and she gasped, "I love it!" We met her in 1984 when we hardly knew a soul in town, and her love of our Kahlua Truffles kept bringing her back to us and helped us get through those times when we had only a handful of customers. We would look out three walls of glass and wonder: Is Kahlua Lady coming? For that, we'd be forever grateful.

For us, life went on.

Justin bloomed in our arms and now he was seven. He never ceased to amaze us, especially when we weren't looking. The year before, from a giant book, he'd memorized the bios of all the U.S. presidents: when they were born, when they served, and how they died, and was now begging his parents for a puppy he could name Jefferson.

Mom doted on her grandson but fretted over his aunt's affairs of the heart. At any moment her love life could be colorful or dull, but either way, Francie was taking a breather, for who knew how long. Question her and she'd hush you. Neither Freud nor Dr. Phil had any answers for poor Mom.

"Why she not want husband? She Old Miss now," Mom complained at dinner, passing a fragrant bowl of *chop chae* past Justin to Skip. Justin couldn't eat chop chae—sesame oil was a no-no.

"Mom, some women don't want or need to settle down. Plenty

of my friends feel the same way," Ginger said, wedging in between Justin and Skip at the kitchen island. Although their home had a formal dining room and an eat-in kitchen, the family preferred to chow down here close to the stove where pots were always simmering. "You just have to accept it, Mom. And, for the record, my sister will *never* be an Old Miss."

"More pasta and beans, Mommy?" Justin asked, holding up his empty bowl.

"Sure thing, Pumpkin," Ginger said. Feeding her son was a special calling. She spent half her life in the kitchen figuring out how to make tasty allergy-free meals for him. By now, she could write a cookbook.

"There's peach cobbler for dessert, Justin."

"With ice cream on top?" he hoped.

"Well, of course, silly!"

Soy ice cream, that was.

In the meantime, Skip's appetite wouldn't quit tonight. "Ever since you and Francie wrote that book about Mike, I can't get enough Korean food," he told Ginger.

Skip was referring to *The Have a Good Day Cafe,* our tale about a Korean family struggling to make a living in America with their shiny food cart. The star of the show, Mike, ends up saving the day with an ingenious idea to replace typical cart fare with a mouthwatering Korean menu. Although we never knew the fate of that memorable little helper who stole our hearts in 1985, our story could only end on a happy note.

"Man," Skip continued, "I literally drool whenever I read the part about the *bulgogi,* so pass it here."

"Skip, don't hog it all." Ginger clamped her hand over the dish of marinated beef strips. "You're not the only one eating."

"Don't be hog," Mom quipped good-naturedly.

Justin giggled.

Skip pretended to snatch Mom's nose with his chopsticks. "Speak for yourself, Soo."

"Skip only think about his stomach," she said, chuckling. "Whenever I would call store, Stella say he is getting lunch."

"Hey, that's not true." Skip laughed back. "I was the food run guy for Stella twenty-four/seven. She bossed me around left and right."

Suddenly, Skip had a memory. A few years back, Stella's lunch order really landed him in the wrong place at the wrong time.

"A large minestrone and a breadstick from Au Bon Pain, Skip, and while you're out, a caffè latte from Starbucks," she had barked from her perch behind the counter.

Air scribbling on his palm from center stage of the shop: "Got it."

"And I want whole milk, Skip, none of that low-fat crap."

"I know, I know. Anything for you, Ruth?" Skip had asked our occasional part-timer. Ruth used to work with Stella at Woodies way back when. Together, they were our very own Golden Girls.

"I'm good, Skip," Ruth said, detangling a bunch of elastic bows used to dress up our gift boxes. Red bows, purple bows, black bows—a thankless task, but somebody had to do it.

"Okay, then, back in a flash."

Upon his return, Stella took one sip of her caffè latte and gagged. "Oh, my Gawd, they used the low-fat crap. Skip, darling, go back and tell them to add the calories, will you?"

At Starbucks, waiting in line, Skip was beginning to feel famished, so afterward he hightailed it around the corner into the Korean food bar he frequented. Their spicy tofu rocked. When he returned to the shop fifteen minutes later with a caffè latte and an aromatic Styrofoam box, our two Golden Girls looked flushed with excitement.

"Why weren't you at Starbucks?" Stella asked, still catching her breath.

"Stella went looking for you," Ruth explained.

"No, really? I was there but . . ." He grew suspicious. "What's going on?"

"Your favorite customer was in," Stella told him.

"The Senator?"

"That would be him."

"Bummer. I'm sorry I missed him."

"Well, Skip, not as sorry as you will be when you hear this."

"What?"

"He brought someone in to meet you."

For months the Senator had been promising to bring a certain friend by the shop to meet our politico in residence.

"So who was it?" Skip wondered.

Stella took a long, orgasmic sip of her caffè latte before replying: "Bill Clinton."

Not as prominent but certainly a character in his own right, Koomo had now been long established as our chocolate barista. He could often be seen outside the shop starting each day with a cup of coffee and a smoke—his "spot o' nick"—before the hustle-bustle of the day began. Rarely could he smoke in peace, though, before a customer got hold of him either to chat, chastise, or deliver a shot glass from wherever he or she just returned, be it Munich or Memphis. Koomo was already notorious for his shot glass collection, hot pepper plants, and funky ties. Typically a loner, his Chocolate Chocolate persona emerged once the doors opened for business, and overnight, it seemed, he preferred the company of our customers more than the Cure in the Tree House. Lovingly, he threatened us at least three times a day: "You guys better stay in business forever. Because I'm here, and I'm here to stay."

"Don't worry, Koomo," we'd laugh him off. "We're not going anywhere."

Famous last words.

Chapter 18

Lemon Heaven

A delicate delight:
white chocolate lemon mousse
with a rim of dark chocolate

It finally felt like we had truly made it. Pick your hour, any hour, and the shop was hopping. Friends and customers hoping for a quickie in the Chat Corner had to take a rain check. Loving every minute of this circus, Francie, boxing Grand Valencia truffles, breathed in. Their citrus essence had her skipping through orchards.

"I swear these could revive a mummy."

Her customer grinned. "That's why I'm buying them."

Meanwhile Ginger was weighing a big bag of Dark Chocolate Cashews sprinkled with sea salt.

"You don't mind if I snitch a few?" she teased her customer.

"Don't you dare."

Between ourselves we were like schoolgirls passing notes, uttering words whenever we got a chance. In our universe, this was the sweetest show on earth: juggling chocolates and customers and hanging out with the ones we loved. At some point it got ridiculously happy in there, feverishly loud, and we had to wonder if maybe, just maybe, chocolate was a drug.

A regular with warm brown eyes approached Stella. "Happy to be back?"

"Ecstatic," Stella replied. "How could I not be? I'm back on the Chocolate Love Boat with my crew."

Koomo quietly cracked up. Watching Stella, who had returned to work part-time a couple of weeks earlier, was like sneaking bubbly all day. During her hiatus, Stella had no choice but to stop looking for love in all the wrong places and had met a nice Jewish boy ten years her junior—Stella's Fella, we called him. With both hips in working order, she was full of swagger and still had her recreational eye out for any Mr. Tall, Dark, and Dreamy.

"Those Lemon Heavens look good," the customer remarked.

Bending down to reach the tray, Stella asked, "How many, dear? A half dozen?"

The customer pondered. "Are they good?"

"*Good*," Francie said, forking one over, "is an understatement."

The customer took the Lemon Heaven between her pearly whites, closed her lips, then her eyes.

Bordered by dark chocolate, its white lemony top was tartly sweet and rich in the way only the best white chocolate can be. Our Swiss Altdorf fiasco with the father-son team happened so long ago it felt like a fable, and recently we decided to revisit that country's finest. Suisse Läderach offered hundreds of pralines with vibrant notes, but with our customers' help, we whittled down our selection to ten miniature chocolates we called Jewels.

The customer purred. "Give me a dozen."

Eavesdropping was Edgar, our endearing eccentric. He hadn't changed much over the years, though his gait was slower and he had a slight forward hunch.

"Hi, Edgar!" we greeted him.

"Hi, Francie . . . Ginger . . . Stella . . . Koomo. So I hear chocolate's good for you now. Every time I open the newspaper, there's another article saying we should eat chocolate if we want to live to be a hundred."

"You're just learning that now?" Ginger teased him.

Koomo, deep in inventory, looked over. "Chocolate, it's not just for breakfast anymore."

"We're practically a pharmacy," Francie quipped.

Edgar chuckled. "Well, then, I think I'll just ask my doctor to write me a prescription for chocolate. In the meantime, I'll have what she's having." He nodded to the customer who had just devoured another Lemon Heaven with an unintentional little sigh.

Chocolate culture was ever evolving. It was 2006 now, and while some of the original customers we held near and dear to our hearts were still around, many customers were part of a new generation of chocoholics, young and old, with progressive tastes for whom organic and local products could be a deciding factor in making a purchase. It was no exaggeration to say that in recent times, the media and the medical community decisively shaped the American chocolate palate, and we were well aware of the movement.

The love of dark chocolate had skyrocketed, thanks to the medical community. Every week, it seemed, yet another news report of its health benefits hit the press. According to CNN.com: "*Chocolate can do good things for your heart, skin, and brain. Scientists at the Harvard University School of Public Health recently examined 136 studies on COCO—the foundation for chocolate—and found it does seem to boost heart health.*"

In the eighties, milk chocolate had outsold dark chocolate ten to one. Now dark chocolate evened the score, and the more bittersweet, the better. With all the great press, we practically *were* a pharmacy.

Once word spread about dark chocolate, interest grew deeper and taste buds more select. Single-origin bean and cocoa bean percentage piqued the curiosity of our customers, so we expanded our dark bar selection to include Vosges, Scharffen Berger, Valrhona, and Chocolate Santander.

Taking chocolate sophistication to the next level was the birth of companies flavoring chocolate centers with the likes of apple liqueur, key lime, and whiskey, then coating them with high-definition tinted cocoa butter more polished than marbles—modern art on a tray. Other companies were making their mark by stirring exotic ingredients into the artisanal chocolate kettle: spices, seeds, tea, herbs, gray sea salt, berries, flowers—even chilies. Vosges's Red Fire Bar was a fusion of Mexican ancho and chipotle chilies, Ceylon cinnamon, and fifty-five percent dark chocolate that had Koomo bragging like the fire-eating dragon he was: "Told you guys I was ahead of my time."

Organic and local were all the rage now, but for us, that was old news. We'd been promoting locally made Naron chocolates since 1984, as well as the organic offerings from Lake Champlain Chocolates for over a decade.

Bottom line: For us, chocolate was, and would always be, a mood thing. As the first establishment to offer a world of premiere chocolate to Washington, D.C., we liked to think we knew what was good, what was great, and what was a joke, regardless of the price tag. A fancy name or box meant nothing, and often a beautiful package that failed to deliver from the inside out reminded us of "The Emperor's New Clothes." We loved bittersweet chocolate, we loved chocolate infused with exotic things, but as equal opportunity chocolate eaters, we also loved quality milk and white chocolate with all the gooey works.

Our philosophy: If it made you smile, it was good for you.

Still smiling on a blissful autumn day in the nation's capital, we were listening to Rod Stewart again. We owned his whole collection of love ballads from *The Great American Songbook* and lately had been playing them all day long. During a lull, Koomo stepped out for his "spot o' nick" while Stan the UPS man dropped off a few cases of chocolate turkeys. After all this time, all we knew about Stan was that he had two dogs, Popeye and Sweet Pea. That's how he liked it.

"Still bouncing between beaux?" he asked Francie.

"You got it."

"Well, you look even prettier now than you did a hundred years ago when we met, Fran."

Stan was one of the few who could call her Fran and get away with it. It was the way he said it, ever so eloquently. She blew him a sleepy kiss.

"Thanks, liar."

The two cracked up.

He nodded Ginger's way. "Hey, beautiful, what's new in your world?"

She yawned. "Not a damn thing."

When the phone rang, Stan shrugged, wheeling out his truck.

"Who knows, maybe that call will bring some excitement."

Francie picked up. "Chocolate Chocolate, how can I help you?"

The voice on the other end asked not for Francie or Ginger but for *Frances* or *Virginia* Park. Her posture stiffened and she hesitated, not liking the voice already. This was no love ballad.

"Frances speaking," she replied formally.

Sisters can hear what others can't. Ginger set down her scissors. Tuned in.

"I'm sorry, who is this? Yes, yes, I'm aware . . ."

Ginger's ears twitched. This was serious business. Not even the sight of Skip in his Three Stooges lounge pants could lighten this moment.

"Excuse me, who is this? Simon who?"

Inching closer, Ginger sensed bad news. Fortunately, Koomo was back to handle a store swelling with tourists. He set out a tray of chocolate-covered pretzel bits.

"Samples, anyone?"

A party atmosphere immediately ensued, but we were in some other dimension.

"Who *is* it?" Ginger lip-synched.

More tourists ushered in.

When Francie got off the phone, we tripped into the back room, huddling far from the madding crowd.

"What's going on, Francie? Who *was* that?"

"The Evil Empire, that's who."

Our eyes locked.

"Ginge . . ."

Sisters just sometimes know. "We lost our lease, didn't we?"

According to Leasing Agent Simon, the Evil Empire considered Chocolate Chocolate its number one model tenant. Not only had we religiously paid our rent on time for over two decades, he told Francie, we were consistently voted their most popular retailer tallied in the Evil Empire's public surveys. But what did it matter when they could tear down our walls, make a bigger space, and collect more rent from a higher-ticket operation? Not only that, Simon could get a fat commission by leasing out our space to someone else. Because they didn't want to lose us as a tenant, he emphasized, the Evil Empire was willing to offer us a lesser space with higher rent in the building, but that would mean kicking out a different tenant—doing to them what was happening to us. No, thank you.

We had two years. Two years sounded like plenty of time to find and build a new location, but we knew better. We were screwed.

The news slowly sank in before we could even talk about it. Remaining silently in the background of our shop, we let it completely sink in until it was time to break the news.

When we told Mom over the phone, her voice was somber. "My cards bad today."

When we told Skip, who just got home with Justin from basketball practice, he was unable to speak.

When we told Koomo, he hugged each of us. Dark at heart, he tried to soothe us.

"Fear not." He repeated his Middle English nonsense: "Ther nys no thyng . . ."

For the next hour or so, even during busy spells, Koomo was on his own. We just couldn't leave the back room, where the sweet perfume of chocolate made us feel deceptively safe. Incubated.

Finally: "Let's take a walk, Francie."

"We need to clear our heads."

Instead, we found ourselves in front of our shop, practically conjoined at the hip and unable to walk away. Was starting over an option? Except for Mom, considerably older but blessed with that forever-fifty glow, we were all well into middle age.

"We're more creaky than cute now, Ginge."

"And Skip's on a senior league tennis team."

"A *senior* league?"

"Guess what their name is."

"The Fossil Fuels? I have no idea."

"Old Bones."

We had been around a long time. That we lasted more than a year in business was a wonder. That we could sleep at night, a miracle.

"Do we have the guts to start over, Francie?"

"Hell, yes."

After a high five, Ginger noticed something. "You seem a little shorter than usual today."

Sigh. "The high heels are gone."

"Oh, no!"

"Think Stella has an extra shoe bag?"

For a while, life went on as usual. Not wanting to alarm our customers, we kept our sad situation to ourselves. When Dashing Dan came in for his gummy bears, we mentioned our orphaned status to him only because he was part of the local real estate landscape.

"Wow, sorry, guys. I'll keep my eyes open, and if anything comes up, you'll be the first to know. Feel free to call me if you need any advice on properties you might come across," he said, handing his bag over to be weighed.

"It's on the house," we said, so grateful.

"No, no." He reached for his wallet, pulling out money and a business card. "I want to make sure you stay in business."

With the holidays nearing, contacting developers for a new space would have to wait until the new year. Until then, we did our homework and researched how the face of commercial real estate had changed in the past quarter century. Apparently, east of us in the old F Street Corridor—an area we once raced through as if bullets were riddling our car—was flourishing now, often referred to as the Penn Quarter or by its Metro stop, Gallery Place–Chinatown. Though aware of the city's revitalization, for all intents and purposes, we hadn't set foot outside our shop in years, at least not much beyond the surrounding blocks of the Golden Triangle.

Basically, it all felt like new territory.

Waiting on customers, we would find ourselves casting an eye at our chocolate shamrock on the shelf. The green box was a bit bent from being knocked over a thousand times, but the shamrock inside still looked new. Glistening.

"Are you thinking what I'm thinking, Francie?"

"I think so."

Maybe our shamrock would bless us with the luck we needed so we could find a new home.

When Ginger's cell phone rang in the midst of Christmas madness, she saw it was Skip. Having an allergic child meant fretting 24/7, and whenever her phone rang, her heart skipped a beat.

"Koomo, can you handle this sale for me?"

"Got it."

She flew to the back room and picked up. For some reason her hand was shaking.

"What is it, Skip?"

"Something's wrong with Mom. I think it's her heart."

The two were Christmas shopping with Justin after school when suddenly Mom couldn't go any farther. She stopped in the middle of Springfield Mall and dropped her bags.

"Skip, help me to sit down."

There had been several recent incidents when Mom seemed to have lost her balance. One time she tripped on the walkway to the house and split her lip open. No matter how hard we pleaded with her to see her physician, Dr. Lopez, she chalked up her incidents to poorly fitting shoes.

"Feet hurt like Stella. I am fine!"

Not this time. Though she put up a fight, she finally gave in and let us take her to the doctor.

Skip's diagnosis was right. Mom's heart was failing.

Tests with both Dr. Lopez and Dr. Pulerwitz, a cardiologist, revealed that she had a blockage in at least one of her arteries and needed to be admitted to Fairfax Hospital the next morning for an emergency angioplasty that would determine the severity of her blockage. More than one blockage meant we were facing open-heart surgery; otherwise, a less invasive stent procedure would be performed. It was the last thing we expected from our youthful mom who had no history of heart problems. She had survived so much in her life that we thought she'd live forever.

Now, the evening before her admittance, we sat with her in her bedroom, praying our only living parent would survive the night. Even Jefferson, Justin's normally yappy Goldendoodle pup, was somber. While she folded her pajamas into a suitcase, it occurred to us that Mom was and would always be, above all else, a brave person. She had survived the Korean War, the loss of her family, and the loss of her husband. She would survive this, too, we told ourselves.

"Everything is going to be fine, Mom," we told her, trying to convince ourselves.

She touched both of our hands. "I live good life."

Her Yamagada cards were nowhere in sight. How come?

"My fate up to God now."

The cardiac surgeon, just before going into the operating room, reiterated what Dr. Pulerwitz had told us. Numb, we sat in the waiting room and held our breath. Unlike Mom, we couldn't imagine eating chocolate at a time like this.

"What do you think?"

"I don't know, I don't know . . ."

Two hours later, the surgeon came out with a smile on his face. Informing us that Mom was a walking heart attack, he also said she was a very lucky woman. One of her main arteries was blocked ninety-nine percent, which was reopened with a stent—thankfully, her other arteries were clear. Then he said the words we were praying to hear.

"She can go home tomorrow."

Our chocolate shamrock was still working.

Chapter 19

Cappuccino Cup

Coffee and cream in a bittersweet cup,
topped with a dreamy swirl
of white cocoa-dusted chocolate

Mom, fully recovered, had a second lease on life and was playing her Yamagada cards more furiously than ever. Often Justin was in earshot, and we weren't sure what our eight-year-old was thinking. But once Mom caught him crossing his fingers when she was calling us at the shop. Perhaps he'd caught on to our New Year's resolution of 2007: Find a new space.

"Any luck, girls?"

"Not today, Mom."

Déjà vu.

Times had changed since 1983. Brokers were oilier than ever; by the time we hung up with one, our cell phones nearly slipped out of our hands. And while we once depended on newspaper listings to help us find available spaces, we now had the Internet. We had Skip, too. One afternoon, tired of clicking and scrolling, he shut the laptop.

"Let's hoof it."

And so we did, day after day, week after week. With nothing in the Golden Triangle area, we ended up looking east to Penn Quarter, considered by many as where the action was. True, lights were flashing, cabs were honking, and sexy new buildings with empty storefronts were everywhere.

But roadblocks stood in our way.

Retail had changed vastly since the last time we looked. Developers had tunnel vision for the cloning of America: Subway, Così, RadioShack, etc. Homegrown independents like us represented a risk. Plus, all the spaces were too big for a cozy sweetshop anyway. Last, and most important, the Penn Quarter area felt like a tourist and nightlife haven, not a home.

"Let's get out of here," Skip said.

And, so, while our window displays changed from season to season, we were on the lookout for a modern-day Oz in the Golden Triangle. In our shop, we carried on from day to day.

Sherry the Southern Belle, our knock-'em-dead attorney, brought in a whoosh of fresh spring air and the sunshine we much needed. "Hi, people," she said with a wave. "I see it's Grand Central in here, so don't mind me while I pick out some treats and treasures."

The Good Son was in, picking out bonbons for his mom *and* his new bride. "Chocolates keep me in good graces with everyone," he told us.

"They're both lucky ladies," Francie said, closing the first box.

Lining the second box with tissue, Ginger smiled; waiting on the Good Son was always a pleasure. Well mannered and cute to boot. "Ready?"

"Not quite," he said, scratching his head. "So much chocolate, so little time."

Skip meanwhile was busy doing his best to help a customer on his first visit in. Tall, salt-and-pepper hair. Stoic, perhaps.

"I need a gift today," the customer said.

"I see you've got your eye on these truffles, here," Skip said. "Let me tell you, they're great."

"What kind of chocolate is used for the ganache?"

Skip laughed. "You sound like a chef or something."

"I *am* a chef."

Usually we were the experts, but not always. And when we weren't, there was always the chance of being grilled. "In these particular truffles, they use Belgian chocolate blended with Vermont cream and butter. You get the best of two worlds," Skip explained, hoping he said the magic words.

The chef mulled. "I use French chocolate in my kitchen. Valrhona's deep, dark baking coins are tops."

Skip sighed, wishing he was in the back room balancing the books with a big lunch from the Potbelly Deli.

"But these sound fine, too," the chef decided. "I'll take a box of four. Can I pick my own flavors?"

"Sure!" Buoyed by the sale, Skip packed up the chef's box with extra care. "Anything else?"

"Not right now," he replied, distracted by the hustle and bustle behind the counter—us, goofing off. "But I'll be back," promised the chef.

Koomo began ringing up Sherry's purchase and expressing his high hopes for his fig plants this year.

"They'd be good dipped in chocolate," she said. "Think about it."

"I agree," the Good Son eavesdropped, halfway out the door. "Let me know when they're in stock."

On her way out, something in the window seemed to slow Sherry down. In the shop quiet, she turned around. Her eyes were red and misty.

"I have to tell you. Remember the chocolate butterfly I bought awhile back? Well, I bought it for a dear friend of mine who happened to love butterflies. She was battling cancer but somehow remained so positive and cheery—my Lord, I'm bitchier on a *good* day. When I gave her the butterfly, she smiled like you wouldn't believe and said it made all her pain go away. She held on to it, always, and wouldn't let it go." Congested with grief, Sherry fought to get the words out. "Her family told me that when she died . . . she was still clutching it."

Our murmurs couldn't quite comfort her.

"Butterflies are special, Sherry," Ginger expressed, recalling Mom and her mystical butterfly.

"Oh, they are." Sherry sniffled, then she composed herself, glancing at her watch. "Gotta go to court, people. It's magic time!"

Speaking of which . . .

One summer day, ten minutes before closing, an unusual man stepped in. Linen jacket, white fedora, and shades of Truman Capote, he seemed to arrive from another period. He looked around. Stalled, like he didn't know what he was doing here. As business wound down, he strolled up to the case. Tipping his hat, his hairless head shone like alabaster.

"Good afternoon. I presume you two are the owners?" His elegant voice conjured up old Washington money. Kalorama mansions, the Cosmos Club . . .

We nodded. "Yes."

"My name is Harold McMillan and I'm a broker here in Washington."

"You're kidding," Ginger said. "You're a broker? I would've never guessed."

He laughed. "I'll take that as a compliment. I'm an artist by night, but my day job pays the mortgage. Helping established retailers find new retail spaces is my specialty."

"So I take it we've talked on the phone, Harold?" Francie deduced. We'd talked to so many brokers names meant nothing.

He pondered as if something uncanny was happening here. "Actually, no, we've never spoken. I was just walking by and something pulled me in here—chocolate, I guess. But . . . is there something I can do for you ladies?"

By October, Harold had shown us a number of properties that held promise, at first glance. But for one reason or another, things never worked out. Not enough foot traffic. Too much build-out required. Rent too high. Ceiling too low. Lease unworkable. At this point, there was nothing new on the horizon. So much for magic time.

"I'll keep looking," Harold said in his tireless way, opening the door for us as we exited yet another disappointing space.

"We only have a year left on the lease," Skip said. "Harold, there's gotta be something out there."

Pause. "There *is* a little space on Connecticut Avenue, a little north of you, that could work. Right now it's a perfume store."

Francie squinted. "A perfume store?"

Ginger squinted as well. "Nope, don't know it."

"Really?" Harold questioned us. "It's just a half block up from your store."

"I know the place," Skip said, not particularly impressed. "It's recessed, right?"

"Yes. The lady who rents it has a temporary lease of sorts. I'm not sure what the terms are. The area's as swanky as it gets, but like Skip said, the space is slightly set back from the street."

"Slightly?" Skip qualified. "It's got to be thirty feet off the main drag."

Harold agreed. "You wouldn't have the exposure you do now, but you'd keep your built-in customer base, being so close to your original location. Take a look, and if you like it, we can proceed. The one caveat is that the owner of the building—who is *not* your current landlord, thank God!—is very particular about choosing a new tenant for this spot. The building is a Class A, meaning, well, it's architecturally superior, and this unusual space is the crown jewel. Go see it, please."

"Thanks, Harold," we said, only half listening. After all, why would a space—both recessed and occupied—tempt us?

With no new prospects in sight, in a moment of desperation we e-mailed Dashing Dan asking if he had any properties available for lease. A couple of days later, his head leasing agent showed us a prime spot on the 1000 block of Connecticut Avenue. The space was spectacular and the rent offered us was below market, but it was far more square footage than we'd ever need. Dan asked the tenant next door if he was interested in splitting the space, but he wasn't. Feeling bad for us, the next time Dashing Dan was in, he scooped out twice as many gummy bears into his bag as usual and handed us a fifty-dollar bill.

"Keep the change," he said.

Our final Christmas, the shop was all dressed up, but before long we'd have nowhere to go. Yet even now, after thousands of faces, new ones still appeared, worthy of nicknames every day—like Francie's new beau, the chef with deep, dark chocolate desires. Earlier in the year, after his first visit here, he had run into Francie in the lobby. She found him disarmingly nice, and the two went for coffee at Au Bon Pain.

"I like being outdoors," he had said. "Bicycling and golf. You?"

"I'm usually indoors, writing."

"Really? Tell me about it."

"Another time," she said, feeling a glow from his interest, "after I hear about all the delicious dishes you plate."

"I make a mean Texas-style smoked beef brisket. Something wrong?"

"Sorry, I don't eat meat."

She wouldn't have guessed the relationship would go farther than a dinner or two, but after a few bumps and even a short breakup, well, here they were: Francie and the chef. Actually, we crowned him Eggman for all the eggs he cracked at Sunday brunch.

"Let's see that ring again," Ginger said.

"It's just a friendship ring, Ginge. Don't get excited."

Ginger tried not to, but, come on, Egg was a keeper. He cooked for Francie and combed her hair. He loved nothing more than when she read to him. And, let's face it, pretty soon she'd be wearing bifocals.

Francie smiled. "It *is* a beautiful ring."

The door swung open and the Good Son stepped in. He took a deep breath. "Got any chocolate here?" He grinned.

Ginger gestured with open arms. "Enough to fill all your dreams."

"Then fill me up a box of your best dark chocolates for the best mom in the whole world."

"Is this the mom who hides her chocolates from everyone?"

The Good Son laughed. "The one and only!" Then he zeroed in on the Cappuccino Cup. "Do you think she'll like this piece?"

"You said she likes dark chocolate, right?"

"*Only* dark chocolate."

"Does she like coffee?" Francie pitched in, passing by.

"*Loves* coffee."

"Trust me," Ginger said, "she'll love this."

The marriage of coffee and chocolate was a match made in heaven. Topped with a meringue-like swirl of white chocolate, the bittersweet cup lent itself to being dropped into a mug of steaming black coffee. Wait for the bouquet. Go cross-eyed. Drink.

"It's always a blast doing business with you," the Good Son said.

"Ditto," Ginger said. "And see you soon, I hope!"

Despite the cheerful season, the year ended on a disappointing note: No new home for Chocolate Chocolate.

Come January 2008, we were back on the hunt, driving around the city in circles one freezing cold Sunday.

"Hey, guys," Skip said, drinking hot chocolate at the wheel, "maybe we should reconsider that perfume store location."

"Why bother?" was our reluctant reply. Perhaps our current location had spoiled us for life.

"It wouldn't hurt to take a look at it," he insisted.

Pulling up to the curb in front of the perfume shop, Skip put on his car blinkers and we went to check it out. Though closed, it was rather darling, what with its convex glass storefront. Still, we wavered. By design, the shop was recessed, easy to miss if you weren't on the lookout for it. On the upside, it was only a half block up the street. We peeked into the dark shop: Its square footage seemed to match ours.

"We'd have to air it out," Francie said. "Chocolate and perfume don't mix."

"What's the tenant's story?" Ginger wondered. "We don't want her kicked out on account of us."

Skip was already on his cell phone calling Harold.

The perfume shop was on a month-to-month lease with no strings attached.

"Sounds promising," we said.

Harold arranged an appointment for us to meet with the leasing agent. Leaving Koomo and Stella at the shop, we braved a frigid, whipping wind up Connecticut Avenue. Hair this way and that. Hollering to hear each other. The property was only half a block away, but this time of year we rarely left the comfy confines of our shop all day, unless it was to run to Au Bon Pain or Starbucks.

"This is impossible!" Francie cried.

"Ugh!" Ginger cried.

Under his 'stache, Skip was chuckling. "Wimps."

In the lobby, warming up, we were studying the building's tenant directory—*The Boston Globe*, HSBC Bank—when Harold arrived. Resembling a character from a Sherlock Holmes novel, Harold oozed French artist in a cape coat and black beret.

"Impressive tenants, wouldn't you agree? And I just heard through the grapevine that *Time* magazine's moving in soon. Oh, there's Mark," Harold said, spotting a young man coming through the revolving door.

Ginger poked Francie. "Wait a minute, isn't that . . ."

"I'm pretty sure . . ."

The young man enthusiastically shook each of our hands. "Nice to meet you all, I'm Mark." Before Ginger could say a word, he added, "By the way, my mother *loved* her chocolate!"

The Good Son!

Our meeting felt like a gathering of old and dear friends. Mark and the company he worked for were the antithesis of the Evil Empire. Walking back to the shop after the meeting, the wind was louder than ever. From her cell phone, Francie called Mom.

"The meeting went great!"

"I know so," Mom said, shuffling her cards. "Lucky eight mean good news."

Back at the shop, Koomo and Stella looked at us like anxious orphans. Both were red in the face.

"I just had a habañero," reported Koomo.

"I just had a hot flash," reported Stella.

For over a year, our poor employees had heard nothing but bad news from us.

"How'd it go?" they asked, prepared for the worst.

Skip nodded. "I got really good vibes."

"*Great* vibes," Ginger said.

"Sweet serendipity," Francie concurred, phoning Egg with a full report while Ginger called Mom with more details.

Perhaps because of serendipity, we soon sealed a deal on a new lease. Beyond airing out French perfume, there was much work to do. We hired an architectural firm to design our space to our specifications and obtain three construction bids. When each one came in higher than the last, our collective gasps could have toppled the Smithsonian. Was building out a new dream store in this age cost prohibitive? More than chocolate, the price tag of construction had skyrocketed since our Sonny Campbell nightmare.

Two people came to our rescue.

First was Ginger's tennis buddy, Buddha. Korean American, too, she'd heard about our woes whenever they went out to dinner, and she came down to the shop one day.

Ginger hugged her. "Hi, Buddha. This is my sister Francie."

Buddha gazed over at the two behind the counter, Francie and Koomo. "Which one?" she joked.

"Me," Koomo primped, "can't you see the resemblance?"

Meanwhile, Francie was shaking Buddha's hand. "I've heard a lot about you."

"Yes, but did you hear that I'm the *third* Park sister?"

Joking aside, Buddha was a serious whiz architect and offered to help redesign the new shop with a frugal eye—her talents shaved nearly forty thousand dollars off each bid. Still orbital but closer to home.

"How can we repay you?" we asked.

"What a dumb question. In chocolate, of course."

The second person to come to our rescue was Dashing Dan. We e-mailed our gummy bear expert to see if he, involved in all phases of real estate, might consider making a construction bid. It was a long shot, but our desperation was peaking. He e-mailed back, saying his company was busy with back-to-back projects but he'd be willing to look at our architectural plans and the three bids to see if he could suggest places to cut costs for us.

Hours after picking up the paperwork, Dashing Dan poked his head in the shop.

"We can do better than this," he said. "I'll have a bid to you tomorrow."

"He'll have a bid to us tomorrow, Francie."

"I heard him."

"Let's celebrate with chocolate."

"Let's wait."

We couldn't afford to jinx ourselves. Instead, we served up chocolate to our beloved clientele until closing hour, trying to steady our hands with every sale. Not an easy feat.

The next day, we went into delicious shock: Dashing Dan's bid came in at twenty thousand dollars lower than the lowest bid. Talk about keeping the change.

High five!

"Time to celebrate, Ginge."

Knife in hand, Ginger was already splitting a fist-sized Peanut Butter Bomb in two. We each took half and bit in. This was in-your-face decadence: honey-sweet peanut butter studded with whole peanuts, propped on a thick layer of caramel and dunked into milk chocolate.

"Hey," Skip was whining, "where's my half?"

"Too late."

"Fine," he quipped with a Popeye toot. Then he went in the back room, seized one for his personal pleasure and ate it whole.

The Saturday before our official move, we threw on our baggy jeans and began the process of transporting chocolate from this space to that. Get a head start, for goodness' sake. Downtown was always quiet on the weekend, which suited our plans for the day. Moods, too. No time for glam or heartache, though. Two large dollies, all the equipment we needed besides muscles, awaited us.

Once upon a time, following Dad's death, we could've moved mountains all by ourselves. Now we were grateful for Skip and Koomo, our two right arms.

Stacking already, Ginger said, "Let's get this party started."

So far October had been bone dry, not a drop of rain. Yet this morning, tropically humid and on the warm side, threatened to give us grief as we pulled off and navigated our dollies, stacked and plastic draped, up Connecticut Avenue. The sky held out.

"Success," Francie sang.

However, on our third or fourth round, just as we were crossing the street with our mile-high dollies, a hard rain began to fall.

"It's a monsoon," Skip declared.

"Run!" we all cried.

Bad idea. Like bumbling stooges, we knocked each other silly. Stacks of chocolate tumbled off both dollies and onto the street.

"Abort, abort," Koomo called out.

The blinking WALK sign changed to a blinking red hand— *30 . . . 29 . . . 28 seconds*—while our soaked quartet tried restacking the mess before any cars got the green light to run over us. But for every box up, two fell over. *15 . . . 14 . . . 13 . . .* To our horror, the winds kicked up and sheets of wet plastic slapped our faces left and right. Francie screamed, hair flat as Moe's. Meanwhile, Ginger was ready to poke out eyes.

"What a nightmare!"

3 . . . 2 . . . 1 . . .

When the traffic light turned green, horns started honking. A cab driver shouted out the window, "Get out of the road!"

"Screw you, jerk!" Skip shouted back.

Moving, after all we'd been through, was supposed to be the last major hurdle—the big sigh—of this nearly two-year saga, but whatever made us think it would be easy? Chocolate, perhaps? Its tonic, even through the most trying times over the past two decades— the bills we couldn't pay, the loves we couldn't have, the dream shop we couldn't keep forever—always had us believing that somehow things would turn out as promising as a Baci love note.

Just as the four of us managed to fill up and steady one of the dollies, lo and behold, it capsized again. The rain kept falling, and the horns kept honking, as if to say, *Losing chocolate in the rain will be the ruin of you!* No wonder we broke into a mad chorus of curses.

"Damn it!"

"Crap!"

"This is hell on earth!"

And then, countering our words of doom, three familiar faces—

customers we'd waited on more times than we could remember—rushed to our sides like charming apparitions in the rain.

"Need some help?"

For the next hour or so, from inside the new shop, locked and dimly lit, we unpacked like a happy quartet about to break into song. Thanks to our customers, not a single bonbon was left in the road. And just as amazing, most of the chocolate, protected by foam and sealed plastic inside the soggy boxes, was spared.

Outside, the rain, relentless if not beautiful from here, grew meditative. Skip was right: This *was* a monsoon.

Once upon a time, under similar skies, a milk boy was making his predawn rounds. On his way home, he fell off his bicycle in front of Seoul's opulent Ban-doh Hotel. From his lowly stance, the boy looked up. Tears ran down his cheeks, knowing there was no one to rescue him in the rain. Still, Dad got up and pedaled for the rest of his life.

And so would we.

Epilogue

October 28, 2008.

Lights out.

We'd known this day was coming; we'd known for a long time. Yet our fate possessed a certain unreality, and it went like this: We aren't really moving. We won't ever have to say good-bye.

Until now.

We were in shock. We couldn't move.

Side by side, we'd spent most of our adult lives in a precious little space that bewitched us when we first laid eyes on it in 1983. Now our eyes drifted to every corner of a shop that, beneath all the years of chocolate love, was still as flawed as the crack in the floor, a crack deep, uneven, and often unsightly. Despite all the grief it gave us, few customers ever took note. Silly us.

Chocolate always took center stage.

All day, Skip and Koomo were in and out of the shop with their overloaded dollies, moving the last of the chocolate to the new location.

During the lunch hour they got by with a little help from our friends: More than a dozen customers formed a fire line, passing boxes of chocolates up the street. But that was hours ago. They needed sustenance.

Koomo, coming in the door: "Got any chocolate-covered kimchi?"

Skip, going out the door: "I'm starvin', Marvin!"

The two had started out cheery, but as the day trudged on, they got weary. Not from exhaustion, from emotion. A dream was ending.

Dad would say, with devout appreciation, that his daughters were touched by the kindness of strangers who became their world. No statement could be truer. His death left a big hole in our lives, and our customers helped to fill it.

There was Edgar, double- and triple-checking his Christmas list, hoping he hadn't scratched someone's name off before his or her time. There was Our Girl Friday, flushed with love. There was Kahlua Lady, eternally letting the cocoa powder fall where it may. There was the Bear, reaching in his pocket for something. So many more faces, enough for volumes of stories.

Skip and Koomo were back. The rude clank of their dollies broke our reverie and it hit us: The party was over.

"All the chocolate's gone," Skip declared.

Yet we could still smell it in here, lingering like chocolate ghosts. Deep, earthy, longing.

"The shamrock, too?" we asked him.

"Gone."

Koomo wondered, "What about these candy cases?"

Scratched beyond repair, they were history. Skip had arranged for someone to remove them in the morning. The rest of the shop—the built-in shelving, cabinetry, sinks, floors—was going the way of the wrecking crew. Our eyes clamped shut at the thought.

"Oh," was Koomo's glum response. His Edvard Munch tie couldn't be more appropriate: *The Scream.*

Skip shrugged. "Well, this is it, guys."

No, no, this can't be it.

"A picture, let's take a picture." Francie dug through her handbag, trembling. "Has anyone seen my camera?"

"Got it," Ginger said, finding it on the counter. "Here, Skip, can you take it?"

He sighed. "If there ever was a Kodak moment, it's now."

"Smile, guys," Skip pressured us.

For a quarter century we had stood behind this counter, looked out and saw the world. In a minute, never again. What was there to smile about?

"Come on," he said, "think chocolate."

Think chocolate? We were nothing like Mom at her moment of doom. Not brave.

"I give up," Skip said, choked up himself.

Koomo, nearly a forgotten figure, took over. "You should be in the picture, too, Skip."

And then there were three.

Framing his subjects, Koomo uttered his gibberish into the camera like Chaucer himself chanting, "Ther nys no thyng superlatif as lyveth a lyf blisful with freends."

"Koomo," we all ganged up on him, "what the hell does that mean?"

As if surprised we didn't know, he translated his oft-quoted line for us: "There is nothing better than living a happy life with friends."

Blinking through tears, we smiled.

Snap!

The minute we opened our doors, our new shop felt like home. The layout and lighting were different here, and the space golden with nary a crack in sight, but the spirit of our old shop, its heart and soul and all that chocolate, came with us.

Even our chocolate shamrock.

But few things in life are as smooth as a Half-Moon Butter-cream Dream. In those last countdown months at our old shop, we had tried our very best to get word out that we were moving, but soon something became horribly apparent: Many of our customers were left in the dark. Our phone, ringing off the hook, was proof.

Where are you?

Where'd you go?

Why didn't you let everybody know?

Our previous Landlord, the Evil Empire, had ordered us to take down the poster signs we printed announcing our move. That was why.

In the meantime, all we could do was hope and pray all our customers would find us as we prepared for our official grand opening party on December 3, 2008, to be hosted by our new next-door neighbor, HSBC Bank. The bank was handling the invitations and champagne, and even picking up the chocolate tab.

Still, Francie was hoping Ginger might consider making a personal contribution. On the eve of the party, she phoned her. The time had come.

"Can I talk you into making some House Truffles tomorrow?"

"House Truffles?" Ginger echoed, confused at first. *House Truffles, House Truffles* . . . And then she could almost smell them, fragrant cocoa-covered pebbles from some primitive cave.

"Ginge?"

Forget the fiasco of dipping eight thousand truffles in one week, forget the fact that her hands never quite recovered. Even if Ginger wanted to make her House Truffles again, eleven years was a long time to store a recipe. Where was it? Could she find it?

"Ginge, are you there?"

And then, like yesterday, all the ingredients popped up on a counter in her head: fresh cream, butter, crème de cacao, pure chocolate blocks, vanilla beans, cocoa powder for the antique finish. She knew precisely what she had to do.

Perhaps that was the sign of a chocolat de vie.

"Ginge, will you make them or not?"

"Only if you're helping," Little Sis told Big Sis.

On the afternoon of the party, we toted in a batch of House Truffles to the shop, truffles as luminous as the Bacis we devoured on an opening day so long ago. Déjà vu! Unless we looked in a mirror, it could've been 1984 all over again, only this time there was something sweet and full circle going on: our sisterhood at any age.

But as dusk fell, we began to fret.

"People better show up," Ginger voiced, dreading a different déjà vu: our dismal grand opening party twenty-five years earlier.

Justin, a big boy at ten and a half, was as tall as his mom now. He put his arm around her. "Calm down, Mom. Some of my friends said they're coming with their parents."

"I sure hope so, pumpkin," Ginger said.

"What about your mom? Is she coming?" Koomo asked her.

"No, she's home with Justin's puppy." Mom and Jefferson were babysitting each other.

Skip, up on a stepladder, was polishing light fixtures. "But *your* mom's coming, right, Koomo?"

Koomo nodded. "Any opportunity to find me a wife and she'll be there."

"Good, that's one guaranteed guest, and Stella's Fella makes two." Ginger did her math. "What about Egg?"

"No," Francie said with regret, laying cocktail napkins in a perfect arc around champagne flutes. "He's gotta work tonight—lots of Christmas parties at the restaurant this month. By the way, Stella and Fella are running late."

"We need bodies," Ginger cried. *"Bodies!"*

With a collective sigh, we went about prettying up the shop.

Next door, HSBC Bank had revamped into an elegant ballroom with tuxedoed servers ready to uncork champagne. Long tables draped in white cloth shimmered with enough chocolate to titillate a small nation. The party, if indeed there *was* a party, would extend into our shop, where two shorter tables were crowned with chocolate and bubbly.

Skip, still on the stepladder, spotted a mob scene headed our way and quickly climbed down.

"Break out the champagne!"

That evening, more than four hundred guests weaved between our shop and HSBC Bank, and there was no time or room for a sisterly sigh, even if we wanted to. Early on, the crowd gobbled us up, and we rarely caught a glimpse of each other for the next few hours. After everybody left, even Skip and Justin and Koomo, when not a single chocolate crumb remained on the tables, we turned off the lights, and in an unrehearsed sister act, sank to the floor behind the counter.

Francie happily exhaled. "I'm dead to the world."

"Ditto."

"So what did Bill-About-Town have to say? I saw you two talking. He seemed intent on something."

"He's collecting letters from schoolchildren all over the country for a book he's putting together called *Kids' Letters to President Obama*. He knew Justin is a history buff and wondered if he'd be interested in submitting a letter."

"Did you tell him Justin followed the whole election, debated with his grandmother at breakfast until the bus came, and named his dog after our third president?"

We cracked up. God, we loved that boy.

Ginger yawned, sleepy, sleepy. "Anyway, if Justin *does* want to submit a letter, and *if* the editors accept it, then Bill *might* ask him to appear on MSNBC with him on the pub date in April."

Francie hummed. A long shot, but you never knew with Bill-About-Town. Magical things always happened.

"By the way, Francie, were you looking for someone tonight?"

"No, why?"

"You looked like you were."

Francie reflected. Ah, yes. Spotting a floppy hat in a sea of guests would've been a nice sight tonight. But even the memory of Gypsy Bess was more than she could ever ask for. "Ginge," her memory jolted, "did you see that blast from the past tonight?"

"Oh, my God, I did! When the heck did Bulldog come back to town?"

"Who knows, but he's looking mighty tame these days. Got a wife and seems to salivate over sweets instead of strippers now."

"He's Pussycat now."

"Living proof that people change."

"Well, so have we, Francie."

"Whatcha mean?"

"No one would mistake us for strippers today."

We laughed.

"Hey." Ginger sat up. "All those House Truffles we made and I didn't get a single one."

"Keep the faith," Big Sis told Little Sis.

Francie got on her hands and knees and began looking for something in the storage area under the candy case. Looking, looking . . . In a bare trickle of light off the street, her excavation was taking forever.

"Francie, what—?"

"Shhh . . ."

Buried deep, some things were worth digging for. In time, Francie pulled out a small cream-colored plate where five or six truffles sat in freshly fallen cocoa powder. *Glinted.* What a vision: chocolate nuggets, unearthed like precious rubble. Ginger caught her breath.

"For us?"

And then, in the beautiful hush: We each took one.

Brought it to our lips.

And let the cocoa powder fall where it may.

Your Very Own House Truffle

INGREDIENTS

18 oz good quality dark
    chocolate

1 cup heavy cream

5 tbsp unsalted butter at room
    temperature

1 tsp vanilla extract

¼ cup crème de cacao

¼ cup uns~~~~ cocoa
    powde~

1 tsp ground cinnamon

2 lbs good quality milk choco-
    late couverture (available at
    gourmet stores)

*A big dose of all the love you've
got to sprinkle and stir in along
the way*

TO ~~~~ANACHE

~~~~ge microwavable glass bowl, combine chocolate and heavy
~~~~ Microwave for 2 minutes and 15 seconds, then whisk until
~~~~. Add butter and vanilla and continue to whisk until velvety.
Whisk in crème de cacao. Pour mixture into a 13"×9"×2" glass bak-
ing dish. Cover with plastic wrap and refrigerate at least 4 hours.

TO BALL GANACHE

With a 1" mini cookie drop scooper, form ganache balls and
place on a lined cookie sheet. Freeze ganache balls for 1 hour.

TO TEMPER COUVERTURE FOR CHOCOLATE SHELL

*Note: Tempering chocolate, a process of heating and cooling choco-
late for dipping, allows the crystals in chocolate to be distributed and
suspended evenly throughout the final product to ensure the perfect*

snap, taste, and beautiful patina to your truffles. If you don't temper, chocolate bloom will occur.

Chop 2 lbs of chocolate couverture into small bits. Place ⅔ of the chocolate bits into a microwavable glass bowl. Set aside the remaining ⅓ of chocolate bits. Heat on half-power for one minute. Take out and stir. Repeat this process at least 5 times or until chocolate is completely melted, making sure not to burn chocolate. Remove bowl from the microwave (temperature of chocolate should be approximately 110 degrees). Stir in the remaining ⅓ chocolate bits (temperature of chocolate should cool down to approximately 85 degrees).

TO DIP GANACHE BALLS FROM FREEZER

Note: This is a messy, but rewarding step; you can use a fork, but in our opinion, fingers work better.

Hold a ganache ball with two fingers and dip into the warm bath of chocolate, covering the entire ball. Shake off excess chocolate from your fingers. Place coated ganache ball onto a lined cookie sheet and repeat until all balls are dipped. Allow your truffles to set for ten minutes.

TO DUST TRUFFLES

For the finishing touch, place half the cocoa and half the cinnamon in a large plastic Ziploc bag. Place half of set truffles into bag and gently shake until each truffle is coated. Repeat.

Serve your house truffles at room temperature, or store in the freezer or refrigerator for future indulgence.

Makes approximately 60 truffles.